THE
FUN
FACTOR

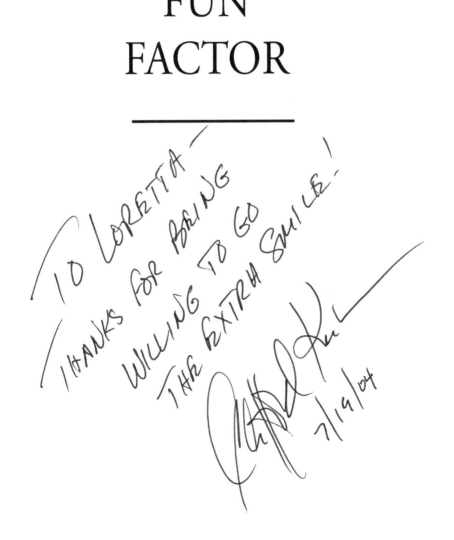

TO LORETTA -
THANKS FOR BEING
WILLING TO GO
THE EXTRA SMILE!

7/19/04

THE FUN FACTOR

*Unleashing the Power of Humor
at Home and On the Job*

Clifford Kuhn, M.D.

M
Minerva
Books

Dedication

To Connie, my collaborator in life-long fun.

Second edition, September 2003

Published in the USA by
Minerva Books, LLC
The Publishing Partner of the University of Louisville
P.O. Box 7311
Louisville, KY 40207

ISBN 0-9723992-5-9

Printed in Canada by Friesens Printers through
Four Colour Imports, Louisville, KY

Acknowledgments

As I wrote this book, countless friends and colleagues offered generous assistance. You know who you are. Please accept this text as a measure of my gratitude for all that you shared.

Some names deserve special recognition. They are Robert Adelberg, Henlee Barnette, Roger Bell, Bill Butler, Steven Carreker, Susan Clarke, Michael Dixon, Larry Dossey, Jerry Eifler, Robert Ellis, Doug Fletcher, Stanley Frager, Liz Curtis-Higgs, Allen Klein, Hank and Page Laughlin, John Laughlin, Caroline Lynch, Nan McDill, Milton Metz, Joe Miller, Gary Montgomery, Wayne Oates, Wayne Perkey, John Henry Pfifferling, John Schwab, Lisa Shuck, Neil Shulman, Robert Slaton, Tom Sobel, Bret Sohl, Stephen Tweed, Patty Wooten, and the members of the Mind-Body-Spirit Group.

To my dear friend Jerry Lewis, whose influence is reflected on every page, my gratitude is deeper than words can describe.

To my children, Rebecca and Gregory, who labored on many drafts of this manuscript, thank you for the joy you give every day, and for bringing to our family your wonderful spouses, Leigh and Michael.

Above all, to my wife Connie, whose incomparable editing skills are exceeded only by her deep love and her magnificent sense of humor, I am yours forever.

INTRODUCTION
by Jerry Lewis

Dear Reader;

You're in for an unusual treat, a treat that is only exceeded by the treat I'm getting writing the foreword to this wonderful book by my friend, Cliff Kuhn.

When I received the manuscript I couldn't wait to read it, and read it I did, twice. And I'm proud to be a small part of what I believe is one of the best "how to" books I have ever read. The "how to" aspect comes from one of the most prolific men of medicine I have ever known. As well as being an expert about laughter and the healing power it can bring, Cliff Kuhn brings us into the broader world of humor that has been either verboten or laid back so far that no one has recognized it. It needed someone like Cliff to breathe some air into it for all to see and understand. In all my years of examining and studying the human condition I have found that it isn't easy for people to truly comprehend humor—its power and complexity—but Dr. Kuhn reduces its complexities into forms that anyone can understand and *implement in their lives.* Just reading about how humor can heal and console when heartaches engulf you is an incredible gift.

The answers the good doctor offers come from years of hands-on experience, studying humor as if he were studying the brain itself. The results of his work are not just for survival, but for real living—ecstacy! The principles are laid out here in 200 pages of a man's life work—a man who cares and loves desperately, emotionally ready for the violent tug and pull of modern life.

Human life is quite funny all by itself. Many men who try to improve it are often attacked and misrepresented. People ask, Why would he bother? How does he know what I need? Why should he care, and for that matter, why should anyone care? The answer is *just because they do*, and people like Cliff Kuhn get more from giving than anyone can really believe. It's right there in the first 40 pages; you'll learn what courage means and what determination means. And when a man like Dr. Kuhn has those two vital elements in his character, that's what makes books like this come alive.

So listen to what Dr. Kuhn has to say. He has a manner that is easy to get involved with. Trust his experience and his tales of humanity, tales that can and will take you to places you only dreamed about. I, for one, learned so much that I feel like I had a semester at MIT, and you will feel the same way, if you care enough about yourself.

After you've read Dr. Kuhn's book, if you think I've poured on the praise too heavily, complain to my attorney, Albert Lasker, 236 Avenue of the Americas, New York, NY 10019, and sue me for misleading you. But if you find I was right, do me a favor and remember the Muscular Dystrophy Association in Tucson, Arizona, or your local MDA office. Thank you.

> Sincerely,
> Dr. Cliff Kuhn's friend,
> Jerry Lewis

Contents

MAKING YOURSELF A HUMOR BEING, 11

CREATING A FEARLESS, HAPPY FAMILY, 32

TRUST AND DISCIPLINE IN A FEARLESS,
FUN-FILLED FAMILY, 49

REWARDING AND REINFORCING THE FUN FACTOR
IN THE FAMILY, 64

MAKING WORK NOT WORK AT WORK, 85

CREATING A FUN FACTOR ORGANIZATION, 105

REWARDING AND REINFORCING THE FUN FACTOR AT WORK,
126

THE CARE AND FEEDING OF YOUR HUMOR NATURE, 145

THE MORAL AND SPIRITUAL GUIDANCE OF
THE FUN FACTOR, 163

THE FUN FACTOR AMID GRIEF AND TRAGEDY, 180

Chapter One

MAKING YOURSELF A HUMOR BEING

A middle-aged CEO sat dejectedly in my consulting room. It was only mid-morning, but he already had the look of a weary man who had already put in a full day's work. His clothing reflected expensive tastes and the wealth to indulge them.

He spoke haltingly. "I thought that when I got to this point in life I'd be happy. I'm making more money than I ever imagined. I've got three homes, a beautiful wife, great kids and expensive toys I can't even find the time to play with."

He went on. "I'm a successful man. I should be free to do anything I want. But I can't get free. I have no time to enjoy any of it. It feels like I'm on a treadmill and I can't get off. I'm trapped by my success and it doesn't make me happy."

I thought I saw tears welling in his eyes. Embarrassed by this, he looked furtively around for a tissue.

"Where the hell are your tissues?" he grumbled. "You're a shrink for God's sake. Surely you have a tissue."

"Do you want a new one or a used one?" I replied.

He looked at me sharply.

"The new ones cost extra," I added, keeping a straight face.

He looked confused. Then he burst into laughter. It lasted for much longer than my silly joke warranted. When he caught his breath, he had a different kind of tear in his eye.

"That's the first good laugh I've had in a week," he said. "I used to laugh all the time. That's what's missing!"

"Sounds like you're not having any fun," I ventured.

"Damn right! That's why I'm here. You're the Laugh Doctor. So make me laugh."

We got to work.

A nervous young woman fidgeted in her chair. It was clear she did not want to be in a psychiatrist's consulting room.

"I'll be honest with you, Dr. Kuhn. The only reason I'm here is because I respect Dr. Adams, my oncologist. I don't have much faith in psychiatry, but she thinks you can help me. She calls you the Laugh Doctor. If you're planning to tell me I can laugh away my cancer, I'll just leave right now."

"I don't see anything funny about breast cancer," I said quietly. "However, I have discovered this to be true. If you can hold onto your sense of humor while you are going through the surgery, the chemotherapy, the fear, uncertainty and pain of it all, you'll do better, live longer and have a better quality of life. If you'll let me, I'd like to help you keep your sense of humor."

"That doesn't make any sense," she countered. "How do you keep a sense of humor when there's nothing to laugh about?"

"That's an excellent question," I said. "I think I know how to help you answer it."

And so we, too, got to work.

These two vignettes are not isolated cases. Both individuals made the same mistake we all make when it comes to humor. They had forgotten the relationship between fun and success; between fun and accomplishment; between fun and adaptability. As a society we are suffering from this same oversight. We have lost our understanding of the true nature of humor.

We think that being financially successful is the best way to bring more fun into our lives. Wrong! We think that fun does not apply to the frightening and serious parts of life. Wrong again! We think that fun is synonymous with laughter and jokes. Strike three!

I'm pretty sure our civilization has lost its sense of humor. We have relegated fun to the realm of recreation and entertainment. We've gradually been depriving ourselves of an essential resource for dealing with the serious challenges we face every day at work and at home.

We've lost our sense of humor for many reasons, and the reasons why are not that important. But it is time we reclaimed it, for as the world's philosopher-clown, Jerry Lewis, once told me, "Without humor, nothing can prevail."

In this book, you will rediscover the nature of your sense of humor—your true "humor nature." You will gain a renewed understanding and appreciation for its power to bring you success in any endeavor. And you will learn many strategies and techniques for restoring the Fun Factor in your work, your family and your life.

Each of us has in the depths of his being an energy so strong it is capable of getting us through the worst experiences of life. Whether it is war, famine, pestilence, disease, oppression or death that befalls us, this energy not only gets us through, but also has been known to lift us above such atrocities in transcendent triumph.

Each of us has deep inside a spirit so universal that it connects us all at a level too profound for words. This spirit sustains our hope and lifts our morale in the face of adversity. It is indomitable.

Within our personal chemistry we carry a medicine that reduces stress and prevents depression even more effectively than any pill.

The energy/spirit/medicine I'm referring to is none other than your sense of humor or, as I choose to call it, your humor nature. To me humor nature is synonymous with human nature, because I believe that humor is the essence of who and what we are as human beings. Our humor nature is the deepest, highest and widest part of us, encompassing everything we esteem about the human character—resilience, perspective, creativity, passion, tenacity, integrity, optimism, hope, and much more.

So integral to us is our humor nature that I believe we could as easily be called humor beings as human beings. For a humor being, *fun is the fullest expression of humor nature.* That is why I say fun is fundamental to excellence in all our endeavors. Without it we are settling for less than our best.

This brings us to a critical distinction. Notice I said fun is fundamental to excellence. I did not claim funny as fundamental. Nor did I mention laughter in this respect. That is because fun is a very different concept from both funny and laughter. Although they may at times overlap, having fun is quite a different experience from being funny.

꩜

I had been performing for almost a week with Jim, a seasoned veteran of the comedy club circuit. One night during dinner Jim asked, "Cliff, do you mind if I ask you a personal question?"

"Of course not," I responded. "What's on your mind?"

"I was just wondering," he said. "Have you ever tried telling the truth up on stage?"

"I don't understand," I countered.

"I notice you tell an awful lot of lies in your act," he continued. "You say things about yourself that I can see aren't true, now that I've gotten to know you."

"But Jim, they're jokes," I replied. "You know, set ups for punch lines. The idea is to make them laugh. Right?"

"I guess I assumed you would have by now noticed the difference between making them laugh and sharing a laugh with them," he answered.

It was an interesting distinction. I wanted to hear more.

He lit a cigarette and continued.

"To me, performing comedy is a lot like a sexual relationship. If two people are technically knowledgeable and competent, if they both know the right buttons to push, it can be extremely pleasurable. But that's nothing compared to the intensity that results when two people make love. I think when you're making the audience laugh, your having sex with them. But if you're sharing a laugh with them, you're making love. And you can feel the difference in the interaction."

"Interesting analogy," I mused.

"I've watched you all this week. You're working too hard at it, son. (I loved it when he called me son. At that point in my comedy career, he was the only comedian I had worked with who was older than me.) The effort shows. You're not having any fun, and when you aren't having fun, the audience isn't either. It's really more important to have fun than to be funny."

Hey, who's the doctor here?

When you stop to think about it, there is a huge difference between having fun and being funny. Funny is a behavior calculated to provoke laughter. Without laughter the effort has failed. Not everyone has the skill to be funny (You know who you are). But more important, funny has relatively limited applicability. In many situations, laughter is inappropriate and unwelcome.

On the other hand, fun is not a behavior. Fun is pure energy, reflecting a certain attitude—willingness. Having fun is never inappropriate. It is a personal choice, a private experience. Whether or not to share fun with others is a separate decision.

Every one of us knows how to have fun. We were born with this precious gift hardwired into our brains. As children, we have fun naturally. The average 5 year-old laughs 250 times a day. Observe a group of youngsters playing and you will undoubtedly hear laughter. Are they being funny? Think about it. When was the last time a preschooler told you a good joke? These kids know nothing about being "funny" and everything about having fun.

We adults were once that way. But then we went to school, where the systems inevitably stifled and suppressed our natural gift of laughter. Do you remember how your teacher reacted to your playful nature? "Wipe that smile off your face;" "What are you, some kind of comedian?" "You think that's funny? I'll show you what's funny!" (This was my personal favorite, because they never did show me what was funny.)

Again and again we were taught that laughter was a frivolous thing and that responsible people were serious. Not wanting to be considered irresponsible, we suppressed our humor, relegating it to the realm of recreation and entertainment, appropriate only when all our responsibilities had been met. Consequently, the average 35 year-old now laughs only 15 times a day.

Reserving your humor nature solely for entertainment purposes is like owning a Mercedes automobile and only driving it to the corner grocery once a week. It could take you so much further. Besides, as it turns out, we have been denying ourselves the full benefit of this marvelous resource based on erroneous information. It appears that seriousness is not at all our most responsible posture. When we are serious, we are not more creative, resilient or healthy; nor are we better communicators. We are all those things and more when we lighten up and take ourselves *less* seriously. Behavioral research shows us that our seriousness has been holding us back.

Here's an example of what we've been missing: About six and a half years ago our family was in a painful crisis. Our daughter had lost her first baby, which was our first grandchild. Six months later, our daughter-in-law, who was also pregnant, went into labor prematurely and delivered an underdeveloped baby who was not breathing.

Little Jordan Kuhn was fighting for his life in the "Premie ICU", while we were struggling with the fear, rage and pain of a possible second heartbreak in less than a year. You can imagine how much tension we had that first morning when my wife Connie and I were allowed to visit Jordan in the ICU. The tension was made only worse by the presence of all the technology—the blinking lights, the electronic alarms, those huge machines supporting such tiny, frail bodies. It was a daunting moment.

At that moment in our lives we did not know what I can now tell you. Later this year our family will gather to celebrate Jordan's seventh birthday. He's a healthy, robust little boy who is currently the star of his soccer team (at least his grandfather thinks so). But we had no assurance of these things on that morning. We were, to say the least, uptight.

As we made our way to Jordan's basinet, Connie saw another baby under an ultraviolet light for control of jaundice.

She grabbed my arm and whispered, "What's that blue light?"

Without thinking, I just blurted out the first thing that came to mind.

"Sweetheart, that baby's on sale for the next ten minutes."

Stupid? Absolutely.

Insensitive? I don't think so (It was heard only by the two of us).

Effective? You bet. It wasn't very funny, but when Connie jabbed me in the ribs with her elbow and whispered, "Cut that out," I knew that the tension had been broken and we were going to get through that experience a little more easily.

That, my friends, is the human humor nature in action; usually not very funny, but marvelously effective in getting us through tough challenges. And it has been serving our species in that regard since the beginning of our history. There is nothing new about the notion that humor is our best resource. It goes back at least as far as the Bible. In the Book of Proverbs we read, "A happy heart is good medicine; a cheerful mind works healing." That's pretty unambiguous.

Sometimes it appears that we have just recently discovered humor's power, because it has only been over the last 25 years that science has taken the matter under serious consideration. Indeed, we've seen an explosion of scientific research into humor over the last quarter century, which has established beyond doubt that it reduces stress, boosts immunity, relieves pain, decreases anxiety, stabilizes mood, rests the brain, enhances communication, inspires creativity, maintains hope and bolsters morale.

Who would not want those benefits in their life? How could they not lead to greater success on many levels? Yet, we seem to have fallen into a pattern of underutilization of our humor nature, a deprivation syndrome characterized by taking ourselves too seriously.

I call this condition terminal seriousness.

Terminal seriousness will take us down if we do not counteract it. That's why we need to reclaim the Fun Factor in all that we do.

The first step in reclaiming the Fun Factor is remembering that we are indeed humor beings who are at our best only when we are having fun. Understanding the distinction between having fun and being funny, we need to ask ourselves frequently, "Am I having fun?" And if the answer is no, we must then be prepared to commit ourselves to having fun above everything else. When we do, we will discover that no matter how much fun we are having, we can always have a little bit more. In Emeril's jargon, we can always "turn it up another notch."

There are specific principles involved in getting more fun out of any experience. These principles work regardless of the circumstances. I have organized the principles into the "Ten Commandments of Fun." If you practice these commandments and make habits of them, you will never be without a reliable way to tap into your humor nature for the energy you need to be maximally successful.

FUN COMMANDMENT ONE: Always go the extra smile.

Don't ever underestimate the power of a smile. Internally, it immediately sets good physiology into motion — muscles relax, your immune system perks up and you feel a surge of energy. Externally, others respond to your smile with encouragement and enthusiasm. As comedian Victor Borge once put it, "A smile is the shortest distance between two people."

All of this takes place even if you don't feel like smiling. So force a smile on your face and keep it there. Just the muscular configuration will cause some changes in your favor. As they say in twelve-step recovery, it makes sense to "fake it until you make it." Or to paraphrase comedian George Burns, when it comes to smiling, "Always be sincere, even if you have to fake it."

Try it right now. Oh, go ahead. Nobody's watching. Force a

big smile on your face and hold it. Can you feel that subtle surge of energy and confidence inside? It never fails to materialize if you hold the smile long enough.

Here is an exercise that will help you follow this commandment. If you are willing to practice this protocol at least once a day, I guarantee you will find it easier to smile more often. That's because when you gently stretch your smile muscles, they become stronger and more available. Hence smiling takes less effort. (CAUTION: THIS EXERCISE INVOLVES MILD EXERTION OF CERTAIN MUSCLE GROUPS. BE SURE TO CHECK WITH YOUR PHYSICIAN BEFORE ATTEMPTING THESE MANEUVERS.)

Exercise #1:

(1) Raise your eyebrows as high as you can on your forehead. Try to touch your hairline with each eyebrow. Hold for a count of 10, then release.

(2) Close both eyes as tightly as you can without hurting yourself. You want to get your cheeks involved with this maneuver. Hold for a count of 10, then release.

(3) Try to touch your earlobes with the corners of your mouth. This should produce the biggest, broadest grin you can muster. Count to 10, then release.

(4) Now try to touch the corners of your mouth underneath your chin, producing a huge frown. Hold for 10, then release.

(5) Gently bring your chin down towards your chest, then look up at the ceiling, then slowly bring your chin back down to your chest. Look up and down in this fashion for six repetitions.

(6) Carefully touch your right ear to your right shoulder, then your left ear to your left shoulder, and gently stretch your neck from side to side six times. Try to bring your ears down to your shoulders, rather than raising your shoulders to meet your ears.

(7) Roll your shoulders in vertical circles, stretching your chest and the muscles between your shoulder blades, for a count of ten. This should feel like a mini-massage.

FUN COMMANDMENT TWO: Tell the Truth

This commandment challenges you to live truthfully according to your personal priorities and values. What is the purpose of your life? Why are you here? Does your daily behavior reflect your highest priorities? Or are you trying to be something or someone you are not?

Admittedly these are tough questions, but if you are going to rely on the Fun Factor to achieve maximum success, you've got to be clear on what's "negotiable" and what's not. Your humor nature will not fabricate on your behalf. Humor always tells the truth, which is why it's so unwelcome in some segments of society.

So if you are trying to be someone you are not, your humor nature will trip you up. It knows and respects you too well to misrepresent you.

Your humor nature is exactly who you are. It is the part of you that you did not create. It is the part of you that you will never improve upon, because there is no need for improvement. You are wonderful just as you are. Why settle for less than your unique perfection?

Be true to yourself. Trust yourself. Get in the habit of asking "Am I being honest with myself?" If you are not sure of the answer, this exercise will help:

Exercise #2:
Sit quietly in a comfortable chair.

Take several deep, relaxing breaths. Try to release all of the tension that will leave you as you let go of each breath. Dismiss all the usual thoughts from your mind and set aside, momentarily, any problems you've been wrestling with. About a dozen relaxing breaths should suffice.

After getting as calm as possible, turn your mind inward and look deeply into yourself. Search every nook and cranny of your inner awareness, looking carefully for any attitudes, ideas, thoughts, or feelings that might be holding tension in you. These ideas and feelings usually come under headings like anger, fear, resentment, judgment, frustration and impatience.

If you identify such thoughts or feelings within you, be

willing to set them outside yourself for the next minute or two. Let go of any anger, even if it's justified. The same for any fear or resentment you may find. Let it all go for a moment.

Then, concentrate on love, peace, joy, compassion, patience and hope. Dwell on these thoughts and feelings for a moment. If, during this moment, doubt or self criticism creep into your awareness, gently set them outside yourself with the other stress-inducing thoughts. Give yourself a minute or two of pure concentration on the many positive aspects of your joyful nature. Complete the exercise by taking one final deep breath in and, as you slowly release the breath, gently open your eyes. Stretch both arms over your head, and then bring them down before getting up from the chair.

FUN COMMANDMENT THREE: Laugh at Yourself First

This commandment is not about losing self-respect or demeaning ourselves. Just the opposite — it is an act of loving kindness. Willingness to laugh at ourselves frees us from the restrictions of the unrealistic and unremittingly harsh expectations to which we hold ourselves when we are under duress. It gives us latitude to appreciate the ever-present inconsistencies and contradictions that are part of our makeup.

Laughing at ourselves helps us recognize the difference between perfection and perfectionism.

Perfection is what we are, and that includes all the inconsistencies and shortcomings. You are not perfect, but you are perfection because of, not in spite of, your contradictions.

Perfection is healthy. It includes imperfection.

Perfection*ism*, on the other hand, is what we think we should be. It is always unhealthy. It is intolerant of imperfection. When we are caught up in our perfectionism, we are brittle and inflexible. We can be broken down by change.

So laughing at ourselves is not a form of humiliation. It is a way of taking ourselves lightly, while still taking our responsibilities seriously. Once we are able to lighten up, we become more creative and resourceful. When the going gets tough, the tough lighten up. If you are having trouble laughing at yourself, this exercise is recommended:

Exercise #3:
Sit quietly in a comfortable chair. Take several deep-relaxing breaths. Try to release all of the tension as you let go of each breath. Dismiss all of the usual thoughts from your mind and set aside, momentarily, any problems you have been wrestling with.

After approximately a dozen relaxing breaths, let your attention focus upon a trait or characteristic of yours that you do not like. It can be physical, mental, or social. It doesn't matter. Just make sure it's something you don't like about yourself. My unwanted trait is my baldness. I put this in an amusing light by claiming to be "a hair transplant donor."

While keeping the trait firmly in mind, try to think of a way this characteristic could be amusing. Be playful and gentle. Do not be unkind or mean spirited. Simply do what you can to see this trait in a more amusing or ridiculous light.

After a moment, discontinue this thought pattern and simply take a few more deep relaxing breaths. End the exercise by taking one final deep breath, slowly exhaling as you open your eyes and stretch your arms over your head, and then bring them back down.

FUN COMMANDMENT FOUR: Allow Your Mistakes
Far from a license for mediocrity, this commandment is a formula for success. If we are to rise above our fear and pain we must have the energy for it. Trying to deny our mistakes and keep them hidden from others is a waste of that precious energy.

As we've already observed, we are perfectly imperfect. Mistakes are inevitable, but they can be real assets if we are willing to learn from them. Acknowledging them freely is the first step in turning our perils into pearls.

What can we learn from mistakes if we're willing to acknowledge them? Of course the most obvious payoff is that they teach us what doesn't work. Being wrong will often alert us to another perspective or point of view. Mistakes also force us to develop new behaviors and coping styles—expanding our repertoire. Tonight Show host Johnny Carson was a master at deliberately "making mistakes" in his nightly monologue as a way of exercising his ad-libbing skills.

Learning what doesn't work, seeing additional perspectives, or developing new coping skills are all priceless assets when we are going through inevitable changes in our lives. And when it comes to expanding repertoires and gaining new perspectives, we have no greater resource than humor.

To practice "welcoming" your mistakes, try this exercise:

Exercise #4:
Be like Johnny Carson. Make mistakes on purpose.

Ask dumb questions. Wear mismatched socks. Push the elevator button after it's already lit.

I call this deliberate foolishness. Acting in this way provides many benefits:
1. You will get used to feeling foolish. It's an exhilarating feeling.
2. You will enjoy knowing that others will misjudge you and feel a false sense of superiority.
3. Being foolish is a good stress reliever.

FUN COMMANDMENT FIVE: Listen Very Carefully

The most difficult thing to do when we are faced with stressful challenges is to listen very carefully. Yet it is a fact that our listening skill is our greatest asset for success.

Most people find listening difficult because they think of it as a passive state. Careful listening may be a quiet activity, but it is certainly not passive. It requires the activation of every sense— our ears, of course, but also our eyes, our touch and especially our hearts.

The goal is to first understand, before seeking to be understood.

If we are willing to listen fully to what we are hearing, we will discover information that will make us more successful. Quite often others will give us clues to the response that will be most effective.

Not only that, but when we listen intently, we will become aware of the humor in a situation that might otherwise be overlooked. This plays right into our commitment to have as much fun as possible at all times.

The following exercise, performed daily, will increase the sensitivity of all your observational senses:

Exercise #5:

Read the newspaper twice.

The first time read the news, comics and whatever else interests you. Then go back through looking for "funny" headlines and captions.

Practice focusing just on the choice and positioning of words, and nothing more. Suddenly amusing variations will become apparent. You can have fun with these variations, which will be missed by the majority of those who read them.

To give you an idea of what awaits you, here are a few examples of headlines that I have found in my local newspaper:

"JUDGE TOLD TO RULE ON LIFE SUPPORT CASE OF MAN ALREADY DEAD"
"KENTUCKY COUPLE CONVICTED OF FRAUD FAILS TO APPEAR AT PRISON"
"SUING EMPLOYER CAN BE HAZARDOUS TO YOUR CAREER"
"INDIANA PARK FEES MAY RISE—OR FALL"
"TOWN OVERWHELMED BY POLLUTION HOPES TO BECOME NATIONAL PARK"
"THIRD TEEN IS CHARGED IN PIZZA STABBING"
"UNWANTED VASECTOMY COULD WRECK MARRIAGE"

FUN COMMANDMENT SIX: Let Go Frequently

In life, as in juggling, success depends less on what we catch than on how quickly we can let go. Failure to let go of what we have already lost increases our suffering and ineffectiveness during life's inevitable transitions.

Now, suppose you are an innocent recipient of misfortune or abuse. You did nothing to deserve the loss. You have a right to be resentful and angry. If you accept it gracefully, you may feel like you are endorsing an injustice or letting somebody or something off too easily.

Nonetheless, it's still advisable to let go and "forgive" as quickly as you can. Do this for one reason only — it's good for you. Harboring resentment, no matter how justified it may be, imprisons the resenter, while making no impact on the situation. It drains energy and limits options. Letting go is something we do for the benefit of no one but ourselves.

But it is not easy. The more important the loss, the harder it is to release our grip. This is where the issue of priorities, raised earlier, becomes important. We must not allow difficulty in letting go of the more important issues to stand in the way of our releasing what we can. Every little bit helps free us to be more resourceful and effective in our responses.

Humor nature provides an effective and practically effortless way of letting go — laughter. We cannot laugh without letting go. Believe me, I've tried and it gave me a hernia.

If you are able to let go, it may be only for today. Tomorrow may require a renewed effort, since resentments have a way of building back up, with or without justification.

Perhaps you will find this exercise helpful:

Exercise #6:
Begin by letting the little things go. There may be things in your life that you can't forgive right now. That's certainly understandable, but it doesn't have to stop you.

To practice this exercise, all we really need is the willingness to release the things that we can. Each little bit helps. Every time we let go of a small resentment we increase the likelihood of eventually being free of our bigger ones.

Start with the easy ones and work your way up.

FUN COMMANDMENT SEVEN: Challenge Your Assumptions

This a crucial "commandment," because most of the fear we experience in life relates to assumptions we make based on past experience or the counsel of others (usually some form of hearsay). We are tireless assumers. Drop us into any situation and the first thing we'll do, whether or not we know the facts, is begin to make assumptions. We are not deterred by ignorance of the facts. Whenever we don't know, we simply make more assumptions, more quickly.

Most of our assumptions go unchecked. Soon we begin to treat them as fact and assign them the power of truth.

There's only one problem with all of this. Most of our assumptions are wrong! Our batting average is so poor it's a miracle our species has made it this far.

In order to survive life's challenges successfully, we need the capacity to challenge our assumptions frequently enough to stop us from veering too far off course. Humor nature is our best resource for this. Challenging prevailing assumptions is the chief mechanism of all humor.

Challenge the assumption that you are sufficiently diligent in riding herd on your assumptions by practicing this exercise:

Exercise #7:

Playing the "What if?" game is a good habit to develop. What and if are the two words that usually begin any assault on your assumptions. "What if .." is a wake up call to your humor nature. Even when you are certain of your facts, "What if .." is still a good habit, because it will stimulate your creativity (eg. What if two plus two did not equal four?)

Practice playing "What if ..." with common every day objects. Look around the room right now and try it with anything you see. What if this pen wasn't a pen? What else could it be? A microphone ... a miniature space craft ... a jumbo lipstick tube?

What if that wasn't my hat? Would it be a frisbee made of cloth ... a lunch box ... a potholder?

Please don't try to be funny in this exercise. There's no need for it. Simply let your imagination run free.

FUN COMMANDMENT EIGHT: **Stay Focused, But Flexible**

This sounds like an assignment for a contortionist. Focused and flexible? Aren't they opposites?

Let me put it this way. We all know the shortest distance between two points is... usually under construction. That's right. The theoretical straight line does not exist in real life.

We are challenged to keep our goals and priorities clearly in focus, while remaining flexible enough to accommodate the inevitable surprises. At times life resembles a game of "Twister." That's why humor is so valuable.

Balance is the issue. If focus overrides flexibility, we become stubborn, rigid and bull-headed. If flexibility eclipses focus, we are left aimless and vulnerable. Humor helps us avoid these extremes.

When it comes to flexibility, your humor nature offers a win/win situation. Flexibility stimulates your sense of humor and humor will keep you more flexible.

If you are having trouble with this seemingly oxymoronic "commandment," here's an exercise that might help:

Exercise #8:

Keep humor props with you at all times. Props are very helpful in keeping focus and perspective.

For example, one prop I find indispensable in rush hour traffic is my red clown nose. When caught in a "logjam", I put on the nose and wave to people in the other cars.

Incidentally, if you should ever want to try this, I will warn you right now that half the people who see you do this won't like it. They'll look away quickly, so as not to encourage you at all. But the other 50 percent love it. They laugh, wave, and tell me I'm #1 - at least I think that's what that finger means.

The point is that, regardless of the effect it has on others, the prop helps me stay focused on the big picture, which keeps the small frustrations in perspective.

FUN COMMANDMENT NINE: Act and Interact With People

The best ideas are merely intellectual curiosities until put into action. Success is measured by action. Life is not a spectator sport.

We must have a plan of action. Even if it calls for us to do nothing for now, planned passivity is better than immobilization by despair. Yes, there is risk involved in taking action. In fact, there is a certain degree of risk in every breath we take. But if we are willing to be bold in putting our humor nature into action, we will find that the risks have been vastly overrated. Others are surprisingly receptive and supportive, once we take the initiative.

Which brings us to the second aspect of this "commandment" — interacting. Nobody achieves success without help from others. Even the Lone Ranger, the quintessential symbol for going it alone, had Tonto at his side.

Have you noticed that your sense of humor becomes stronger the moment it connects with another person? Amusing yourself is better than nothing. Sharing your humor with others is the best. You will find that if you make the effort to reach out with humor, others will be eager to meet you more than half way.
Here's an exercise to help with this challenge:

Exercise #9:
Reach out. Engage other people at every opportunity.
A childlike, playful spirit is the best approach. Despite the impersonal tendencies of modern technology, there are many everyday situations in which we find ourselves in close proximity to other people. Do we interact? Usually not.

A prime example is a ride in an elevator. Here we have a small room, many people, and no windows. So what do we do with this golden opportunity to interact? We stare silently at the numbers over the door.

Don't ever let this happen to you again. Say something - anything. Break the silence.

My favorite ploy is to announce, "If I'd known so many were coming to this meeting, I'd have reserved a bigger room." Then I'll ask for somebody to give the treasurer's report. Someone usually "volunteers", and has some fun with it. I'll ask departing passengers how they want to vote on the upcoming merger issue. Newcomers are greeted with, "You missed the first part of the meeting, but don't feel left out. We elected you president." By the time we've gone a few floors, everybody's smiling and having fun. It's silly. But it's better than staring at the numbers.

There are many similar situations. It's ludicrous to be thrown into face-to-face contact and have nothing to say to each other. Don't let it happen. Reach out. You never know whom you might meet.

FUN COMMANDMENT TEN: Celebrate Everything

Perhaps you've heard the story of the optimistic little boy who, when confronted with a room full of horse manure, dove right in, exclaiming, "With all this manure, there's got to be a pony in here somewhere!" Although I don't think I want to hug him right now, I think the little fellow's got it right.

No matter how big a pile of "manure" life dumps in your path, looking for the pony is the best response. Even if there is no pony, digging in with enthusiasm is better for us than being burdened with reluctance and resentment. Between you and me, there usually is a pony, but we miss it because we're not looking for it.

When you opened your eyes this morning, you were already breathing. If not, I don't think you should be reading this.

If you went on to check the obituaries and didn't find your name, you're apparently alive. That's a miracle. Celebrate it.

Celebration is made up of two elements — gratitude and joy. Remember, joy is the most natural state for us humor beings. If you want more joy in your life, begin each moment with gratitude. Gratitude is the essence of celebration. It doesn't have to be noisy or raucous. A quiet "thank you" to a special person in your life can be an effective form of celebration.

If you have not been celebrating everything, try this exercise:

Exercise #10:

Get in the habit of listening for the sounds of laughter constantly going on all around you. I call these sounds the Symphony of Laughter.

Whenever you are out in a public place, such as the mall, an airport, or a theater lobby, you can hear laughter, because that's the way we communicate when we have no imposed agenda. Whether it's a giggle right beside you or a guffaw from across the room, the sound will lift your spirits and bring a smile to your face.

Soon one more laugh will be heard—yours.

There you have my Ten Commandments of Fun, each a practical strategy for bringing forth your humor nature in all its strength and glory. Notice that all of them are focused on you, rather than the things going on around you. That's because, if you're aiming to focus on fun, you must look to yourself first. As selfish as that may sound, it's simply the way it is.

The roots of fun do not lie in the circumstances or things that surround you. They are deeply embedded within your being. If you catch yourself thinking thoughts like, "I could have more fun, if I had more money" or "My job would be more fun if the boss would get off my back," you're focusing in the wrong direction.

Fun starts inside you and works its way out. It doesn't happen the other way.

The best way to remember how fun works is to "take" my Ha Ha Ha Prescription. Whereas most doctors say, "Open wide and say AH," I say, "Open wide and say HA HA HA."

The first HA is Humor Attitude. This is where fun begins. Attitude is a 100 percent inside job. Our attitude may be the only thing in life over which we have total control. If we cultivate an attitude of willingness to be light and playful, to appreciate all the absurdities swirling around us all the time and to laugh whenever we can, we have done our part.

The next step happens automatically, without any effort from us. Our Humor Attitude creates a Humor Atmosphere around us. That is the second HA. It just "oozes" from us. Others may not know what to call it, but they know it's there. They can feel it. They are drawn into it. It's irresistible. They want to be near us and hear what we have to say. They are eager to share their positive thoughts with us. They want to "play" with us.

Once this is accomplished, what follows is a no-brainer. The very next thing we do will be fun. That's the last HA—a Humor Action. Humor Action does not require anyone to be witty or funny. There is no pressure to perform or to make anything happen. It is merely a trustworthy natural outcome.

Because we have the tendency to mistakenly think that success produces fun instead of the other way around, we often find ourselves trying to apply the HA HA HA Prescription backwards. We attempt to say or do something funny (Humor Action) hoping that our "performance" will stimulate laughter (Humor Atmosphere) and thus lighten the mood of everyone present (Humor Attitude).

It doesn't work that way. Even when it seems to, it's only a transient phenomenon, hardly a dependable basis for lasting success. Sustained excellence comes only from having fun first, and that begins, not ends, with attitude.

With the HA HA HA Prescription and the Ten Commandments of Fun under our belts, we are now ready to consider how to build the Fun Factor back into our lives. Let's begin by looking at the most basic social structure we encounter in life— our family.

Chapter Two

CREATING A FEARLESS HAPPY FAMILY

The human act of procreation being what it is, it would strain credulity to make the claim that we were all conceived in fun. However, one could infer that it's supposed to happen that way. Sperm seeks union with egg in a moment of passionate release, clearly designed to be ecstatic.

Such is the spirit attending the inception of each of us humor beings. What happens next, for better or worse, is the process of family, that confluence, more or less, of individuals into which we are born and raised.

Much has been written about the ideal mix of persons, roles and genders that provides the best family experience. Discussions abound weighing the relative merits of single parent versus two parents, or only child versus many siblings. But what everyone acknowledges without question is that the presence of family, surrogate or other, is essential for normal growth in the early years of life.

Family is the foundation of our self-perception and our veritable launching pad for life. It is in the intimacy of family that we first learn what to value or despise about ourselves. The humor being's need for family is so great that, when it is lacking, it is considered to have pathologic consequences on subsequent development.

One of the reasons for family's essential role is that the earliest interpersonal communication in life takes place within its context. When we are approximately two months old, after finally gaining sufficient muscle coordination to focus our eyes and control our facial muscles, we look up at the person hovering over us, and smile. It is not gas. It is a genuine smile. It is our way of saying "Hi," long before we have words or even thoughts. It is a sacred moment of humor nature. You may not remember that far back, but chances are the person who received your first smile has never forgotten it.

Steven, a 52-year-old man suffering from chronic unremitting back pain, was reporting on a recent trip he had taken to visit his 10-week-old grandson for the first time.

"The first morning, I was sitting in the living room, having a second cup of coffee, when my daughter brought the little fellow in to see me. She asked if I wanted to hold him. She didn't have to ask twice.

"He was so small. It had been a long time since I'd held a baby in my arms.

"I was looking down at his sweet little face when he opened his eyes and looked directly back at me. Then he smiled.

"They said it could have been gas, Dr. Kuhn, but I know it wasn't. It was a smile. It was like the roof had opened up to let sunshine directly into the room. I felt a wonderful warm feeling all through me. I smiled back and we really connected.

"Then I noticed something. My pain was gone. Dr. Kuhn, the pain never leaves me, but, for just that moment, it disappeared completely. It was a miracle."

That's the power of our first smile, which illustrates how naturally inclined we are toward humor, right from the outset. Like it or not, that's just how deeply humor nature is embedded in our character. This is why I believe it is absolutely crucial for every family to decide how it will handle the issue of fun. The fact that humor will emerge is a given. The only decision is regarding how it will be received.

What will be the response to that first smile? Will it be welcomed? Will it be returned? These are critical early questions, which will form the foundation of family interactions for years to come. Since our humor nature is so integral to who and what we are, we are extremely vulnerable, especially early in life, to the manner in which the family embraces fun. Will it be healthy or unhealthy?

Put another way, humor has the capacity to cut deeply. As such it can, from the earliest moments, bring us closer together or drive us further apart. Is it to be used in the family to relieve pain and suffering, as in lancing a boil? Or will it serve the purpose of causing pain and injury, as in a stabbing attack on vital organs?

There is another element woven into the fabric of that momentous first smile. It is the spirit of fear. As infants we are helpless to fend for ourselves. If our smile cannot engender good will and encourage a nurturing protective response from those in charge, we are in dire straights. It is clearly a matter of survival or annihilation.

For the adult it is also a fearful moment. To hold in our hands a life so helpless and dependent upon our skills and judgment, to be the recipient of that degree of trust, to feel that depth of responsibility, is a daunting experience. Fear is definitely in the air.

And so we must choose in that instant, and in the countless similar instants that will follow, whether we are going to be guided by the fun or the fear; the smile or the impending panic. We cannot follow both, because they are mutually exclusive. Fear is devoid of fun, while fun is essentially fearless.

As Steven's experience indicates, choosing to respond in fun rather than fear can make for a healing moment that will sometimes seem miraculous. Incorporating this choice into the ongoing style of family interaction insures that these "miracles" will occur with welcome frequency. Such moments do add up over the years.

If the smile is welcomed and honored as the basis of family interaction it creates a fearless happy family. What would such a fun-based family look and feel like? The atmosphere would be supportive, welcoming and nurturing. It would be a safe place for all members—adults as well as children. There would be open communication. Honest expression of feelings would be not only tolerated but respected and honored. Play, being the natural learning tool that it is, would have a prominent role in the family routine. Humor would "forgive" a multitude of mistakes. Perfection would be celebrated; perfectionism discouraged.

A grandmother was standing on a lovely beach with her three-year-old grandson, the apple of her eye. Both were enjoying the magnificent waves and the salt-water spray.

Suddenly a massive wave swept the little boy from her grasp and carried him out to sea. Beside herself, the grandmother fell to her knees, beseeching God to save her beloved grandson and, if necessary to take her life instead.

In the midst of her desperate prayer, another wave crashed in, depositing the little fellow back at her side, soaking wet, but otherwise unharmed. (That's perfection.)

She looked at her grandson, then back up to the heavens, and said quietly, "He had a hat." (That's perfectionism)

Beginning with the infant's earliest smile, a family committed to sustaining and supporting the Fun Factor will find it has a vast array of humor communication options available as time goes on. A smile, though perhaps the most durable, is by no means the only choice. Stretching from the subtlest to the most intense, there are no less than 16 different expressions that can be used to communicate humor and fun. All of them deserve to be included in the family arsenal.

There is the smirk, which is the subtlest expression of humor known to mankind. It involves a very slight broadening of the mouth and the gentlest hint of openness in the eyes. Only those who are intensely looking for it will ever see a smirk.

Next is a smile, silent, but, as we have noted, quite profound. A smile is non-intrusive, but nonetheless easily noticed. The corners of the mouth are up-turned and there is a sparkle in the eyes.

One step up from a smile, we find the grin. Grinning is really a smile into which additional facial muscles have been recruited. The corners of the mouth are stretched upward and outward. The cheeks are involved and the eyes are narrowed and "soft." With the broadest grin, the ears actually tilt back.

The next step is a snicker, which is the first audible level of humor expression. A snicker is sort of a grin accompanied by staccato bursts of air released from the nose. It's also useful for clearing out sinuses.

A titter is nothing more than a snicker that has found its voice. As such it is slightly louder and higher pitched than its predecessor. At this point we are approaching the upper limits of voluntary control. A strong titter can be difficult to suppress.

A breakthrough is achieved with the next gradation—the giggle. This delightful expression combines all of the previous steps and adds a deeper louder voice, involving the neck and chest ever so slightly. When we reach this level of involvement, our humor nature is capable of taking over completely. We have all experienced the frustration of attempting to suppress a giggle. The harder we try, the stronger the giggle becomes, often to our utter embarrassment.

Moving up the ladder from a giggle, we encounter the chuckle, which resembles the sound of a dog whose bark is caught in his throat. The chuckle is distinctly louder than its predecessor, but its sound may not be detectable beyond the confines of a relatively small grouping of people. The sound of the chuckle comes primarily from the back of the throat.

The chortle is an escalation of a chuckle in both volume and depth. Think of Ed McMahon's responses during Johnny Carson's monologues on the Tonight Show. That's a chortle, a sound that originates from deep in the chest and is loud enough to fill a room. Santa Claus is another famous example of the chortle in action.

At last we reach the level of a laugh. You may previously have used this term more generically, to describe almost any expression of our humor nature, but now that you have a connoisseur's appreciation of the menu, you can be more precise. A laugh is an energetic and rhythmic expression of amusement that involves the head, neck and torso.

By the time you have reached the level of laughter, you are no longer in control. Laughter is not only unrestrained, but also infectious. You cannot help but go along with it. The sound of laughter comes from deep in the chest, but unlike the chortle, it has an unrestricted range and volume. A laugh has a definite rhythm and is often quite melodic. It has been said that laughter is God's music. But, there's more—much more.

Turning the dial another notch higher, we encounter the cackle. A cackle is a laugh on pep pills—more energetic and higher pitched than its predecessor. If the torso isn't already shaking with laughter, it surely gets a workout with a cackle.

The next gradation in humor expression is a guffaw. When things reach this level of intensity, the entire body is involved—arms, legs, and sometimes certain sphincters. A guffaw is loud and strong. It is incompatible with a full bladder.

The guffaw is probably the strongest humor expression we make by ourselves. However, if we are in the presence of other people, there are even more intense experiences to be had.

A howl and a shriek are the next escalations. Both communicate a sense of being overwhelmed by fun nearly to the point of saturation. When we have reached the level of howling and shrieking with others, it's as if we're saying, "Enough! Let us catch our breath. We can't laugh any harder." But we can.

A roar is a group phenomenon. Individuals may howl and shriek when they are intensely amused, but only a crowd can roar. When we are swept up with roaring laughter, individual differences are momentarily lost and we are all of one mind and voice.

Yet there is still a higher point to be reached. To convulse in laughter is the most all-encompassing expression of amusement. Every part of our physical being is overcome by laughter. We have lost control completely. If you are standing, you must sit down. If you are already sitting, you are likely to end up on the floor. If it hasn't happened already, now is when normal continence is lost.

Which brings us to the epitome of laughter intensity—the act of "dying." "I died laughing", is one way we describe this incomparable experience. The term is, of course, used figuratively, but the allusion is apt. Once you have experienced this level of laughter, you are physically and emotionally spent. You have nothing left. In the moments that immediately follow, you experience a rebirth of sorts. Like a newborn infant, you may be physically weak and lack coordination. All of your senses may be refreshed and sharpened. And, in some instances, you may need a change of underwear.

Lest you think these latter more intense humor expressions don't fit within the confines of a family, allow me to share a story reported by Betty, a participant in one of my recent Fun Factor workshops. Note the evidence of guffawing, howling, convulsing and "dying," all taking place in a family kitchen, to the benefit of everyone present:

"This week my husband and daughter were standing in the kitchen while I was making a cake. Out of the blue, my husband said to my daughter, 'Did you know, if you sneeze, fart and cough at the same time, you will die?'"

"I said, 'You will what?'"

"You will die," he repeated.

"At that moment I began to laugh so hard I was squealing. Tears were running down my face. I couldn't stop and, when I would try to stop, it would start up again. I began to stagger around the kitchen like a drunken person, still holding the batter spoon. Everyone was laughing so hard and, oh, it felt so good.

"Actually what triggered the whole thing was remembering a girl in high school who had done two of the three, and I was visualizing the scene all over again. I couldn't imagine her doing all three. She probably would have just fallen out of her chair."

It would seem a vast expanse between the silent, yet profound, first infant/parent smile and that raucous kitchen scene described by Betty. How can it be done? How can a family traverse that distance, while maintaining the stability and decorum necessary for teaching discipline and other crucial life skills?

It can be accomplished only through the commitment of the grown-ups in charge. Family is, after all, a collaboration of adults committed to sustaining a network of relationships dedicated to the welfare of the next generation. As such, the adults must call the shots regarding the role humor will play. Even though the infants are likely to be in closer touch with their humor natures, it is up to the adults to set the tone.

We know that the overall health and vitality of any family is principally determined by the health and vitality of the adult relationships by which it is built and maintained. The values and characteristics of succeeding generations are clearly inspired by what children observe and experience as they witness the interaction of the parents and adults in and around the home. Thus, appreciating the benefits of humor in the parental interaction is the first step in recommending it for the entire family.

Few would dispute the observation that an intimate, committed and supportive relationship between two adults has a beneficial effect on the health and happiness of both. Put simply, it has been well documented that married persons live healthier and longer lives, although some might argue that it only seems longer.

What might humor have to do with all this? Research has demonstrated that marriages are more stable and enduring when each partner possesses a strong sense of humor and is willing to use it. Lefcourt and Martin (1986) studied the role of humor in a large sample of marital relationships and found that laughter was positively correlated with increased engagement as well as increased non-destructive interaction. In other words, laughter enhanced intimacy and mutual trust, while decreasing the incidence of destructive and violent exchanges.

Therefore, even before there are children around to observe and participate, the adults in a family unit would be well advised to exercise their fun-loving humor natures liberally, and to develop mutual trust in fun as a means to strengthen and sustain healthy relationships. By doing so, they will not only benefit their immediate plight, but will also ensure that humor has a natural and respected role in future family transactions. Then, as offspring emerge, the parents will serve as models for fun, long before they have the chance to articulate their attitudes verbally.

Thus the roots are laid down long before the infant is capable of words or even thoughts. Later when events register with more memorable clarity, there is a non-verbal understanding that fun is a positive element, capable of bringing healing reassurance to otherwise anxious moments.

My first recollection of humor "saving the day" in my family occurred when I was about 4 years old. I had been outside playing in our backyard one afternoon, when I came into the house for a drink of water. I walked through the back door right into our kitchen and directly into the middle of a fierce verbal exchange between my mother and father. They were really angry at each other and I was stunned. I had never heard them talk in such tones.

Just as I entered the room, my mother shouted her final angry phrase at my father, and then stomped out of the kitchen, slamming the door behind her for emphasis.

My father, sensing my distress, didn't hesitate an instant before he made as if to follow her, walking right into the door she had just slammed shut.

This bit of impromptu slapstick on my father's part made me laugh at the time. And it "told" me, better than any words could have, that things were not as bad as they appeared, and that we would get through this upheaval in good shape.

It was very reassuring. But the groundwork had apparently been previously laid to define his antic as an acceptable behavior at that critical moment. If he had stopped to calculate the move, the healing impact would have been compromised. By the same token, had I not been exposed to perhaps countless previous examples of my father being silly, none of which are in my conscious memory, I would probably have been incapable of accepting it as reassuring.

From the point of view of the child, it is important that the parents not be heavy-handed during those early foundation-building years. We've noted in passing how fragile and vulnerable the infant is when expressing his/her fundamental playful nature. Any response that communicates rejection and disapproval, such as shaming or ridiculing, can have a devastating effect on self-esteem and self-confidence.

On the other hand, the budding self-image is equally vulnerable to overly aggressive attempts to introduce humor. So fragile is the child's humor nature, it can be likened to a campfire being built from kindling. If the fire builder lacks sufficient patience to nurture the small flame by adding appropriately sized twigs and instead prematurely introduces too large a log, the fire can be snuffed out.

This analogy holds as well for the ongoing maintenance of fun as a valued family resource. Once a fire is going well, the work of the fire builder is not done. Constant effort is still required to oversee, and add new logs as required to keep it going. Similarly, a vibrant humor atmosphere needs frequent encouragement. If neglected, it will quietly fade into nonexistence.

Hence the concept of play becomes instrumental in creating a fun-based fearless family. Play is the natural exercise of healthy humor. Children play easily, but parents may have to remember what it is and how to do it. First and foremost, it is important for the adults to understand and for the children to learn that play at its best is not an evasion of responsibility. It is just the opposite—an exercise in learning effective coping skills for challenging circumstances. As such, play can be the most useful teaching and learning tool the family has.

Play is an essential component of the daily interaction for a fearless happy family, but every member must understand and abide by the parameters. Here are a few simple rules of engagement for family play:

1. <u>Play is collaborative.</u> Laughter is with, not at, one another. This rule speaks to the issue of mutual respect, perhaps the single largest stumbling block to successful family fun.

Too often adults will misuse humor to embarrass or ridicule the children. Even if this proves to be funny, it is not fun for the youngsters involved. For them, fun becomes associated with discomfort and failure. If the point of having fun is to create an atmosphere for learning, the "playing field" must be relatively level. On the other hand, the most common fear that parents have when they consider "allowing" more play, is that the children will lose respect for their authority and throw the family hierarchy into turmoil. After all, someone has to make the rules, and it should be the adults.

That's why we use the term mutual respect. It cuts both ways. Children must understand that playful interactions do not change the reality that parents are in charge of and are responsible for the safety and well being of the family. When fun involves disrespect for this reality, it should be treated as an abuse that cannot be tolerated.

2. Family play should be all-inclusive, not excluding anyone who wants to participate, except for disciplinary reasons.

An atmosphere for fun enhances family unity only if the fun is open to all members. When there are "haves" and "have nots," rivalries spring up, competing for attention and affection. This soon deteriorates into a fear-based spirit of interaction.

3. Family members play family "games" by choice, not coercion.

Even though fun is the natural tendency of humor beings, no one should be forced to participate in play against his will. For one thing, there are times and situations that require a serious demeanor. There is an important lesson to be learned here. Life is not all fun and games.

For another, when a person is forced to play against his will, it amounts to little more than a form of hurtful humor, demeaning and often humiliating the victim.

4. Family play should be as non-competitive as possible. The process of having fun should always take precedence over "keeping score."

Ideally, when fun is promoted in a fearless happy family, there are no losers. The goal is to incorporate everyone in a joyful interplay that celebrates and nourishes growth. Learning to trust and enjoy the moment-to-moment opportunities for spontaneous candor, regardless of the eventual outcome, prepares youngsters for a healthy "one-day-at-a-time" approach to life. Focusing upon process, teaches the value of quality over quantity.

5. All players should respect the rules and treat their playmates fairly, although creativity is always encouraged.

Game play is the modality through which the fearless happy family provides models for values and fairness. In an atmosphere of fun, children can explore the consequences of cheating, hopefully learning that the greater satisfactions lie in meeting the challenge to excel without breaking the rules.

6. Despite its many recognized benefits, play is a privilege, not a right.

All members of the family, especially the children must understand that participation in family fun is a privilege to be earned and maintained by living up to certain standards of conduct. Misbehavior may result in exclusion from playful interaction for a prescribed time. By denying this positive experience in response to unacceptable behavior, the fun-based family creates an incentive to change behavior, without resorting to fear-based alternatives.

7. It is understood that playtime has a definite beginning and end.

By encouraging playfulness the family hopes to teach principles and behaviors that will bring success in the world at large. One such skill is the ability to make judgments regarding the appropriate balance between work and play and to exercise the discipline to maintain that balance.

8. The chief objective of play is to teach responsible behavior, teamwork and discipline.

The concept of discipline is critical. Though the ambiance of family play is collaborative, it does not imply an absence of discipline. Mutuality in having fun is not a license to ignore the reasonable lines of authority. In fact, using playfulness to escape responsibility or accountability is as much an abuse of humor as sarcasm and ridicule. Such tactics should be discouraged.

But if a parent has a strong need to be in control at all times, he will not encourage a fun based atmosphere. He will choose a more rigid authoritarian stance, which is in reality fear-based. As a result, the family will be the very antithesis of the fearless happy unit we are advocating.

It is important to note that humor may be used to support either the collaborative or the authoritarian style mentioned above. We have previously recognized that it can be employed to heal or hurt, depending on the intent of those in charge. In the fun-based family, humor is used only to heal.

~)

I was about five years old when, one afternoon while my father was taking a nap, I fell and bit my tongue so forcefully that it split down the middle.

Blood flowed freely as my mother scooped me into her arms, yelling for Dad to wake up and drive us to the emergency room. As we raced out to the car, Mom holding my tongue together with a washcloth, I remember two things as vividly as though it was yesterday.

One was the fearful thought that I was going to lose my tongue.

The other was the sight of my Dad, not yet completely awake, running out of the house without his pants on.

When he had to go back for his pants, Mom and I both laughed, and my fear diminished.

Inherent in this vignette is the unspoken understanding that it was safe to laugh, even in a moment of distress. My father was a natural clown in many ways. As if by pure instinct, he could usually be counted on to effortlessly do or say something that would ease tension with laughter. That gift was not unique to him. It is simply the humor nature that lies within us all. Unfortunately it goes to waste in many families for lack of a clear consensus that it is acceptable and even desirable to laugh with one another.

I was lucky to grow up in a household that was ruled by such a consensus. As I carried it forward into my own family, my wife initially had reservations. She had uncomfortable memories of sarcasm and put-down humor amongst her siblings. She thought that playful silliness between parents and children lacked dignity and threatened decorum. Her concern was that the children would become disrespectful, if encouraged to laugh at and with us.

Had I not had the experiences from my childhood to reassure us I might have given in to her fears. We are both glad I didn't. Little did we know that the Fun Factor would be the glue that would hold our family together during extremely difficult times.

By the time I graduated from medical school we had begun our family. Five years later, as I finished my psychiatric training. Our family was complete. We had a son, aged 5 and a 3-year-old daughter.

Looking back, I can see now that I was overwhelmed by the responsibilities I had taken on. Not being the brightest member of my medical school class, it had been necessary for me to struggle just to hold my place in the middle of the pack. Now, uncertain of my skills, I had three people depending on me to be successful, not to mention the many patients who were lining up, expecting me to have answers and the cures for their diseases. I felt like I was in over my head.

That was when I turned for relief to alcohol. At first it was for an occasional buzz that would allow me to forget temporarily about all the pressure I was feeling. I suppose it would have been fine if that had been all there was to it. But, as you have probably guessed, it didn't stop there.

In just a few years' time my drinking escalated to the point of my needing it every day. Though I wouldn't admit it until many years later, I was addicted to alcohol. Daily drinking remained a necessity for the next 20 years.

They call me a "high bottom" drunk, which means that although I occasionally embarrassed myself at social events, I was never arrested for public intoxication, never missed a day of work because of alcohol, and didn't lose my job or my family. Publicly, I was relatively unscathed. This did not hold true for our family life. As is generally the case with alcoholism, within the private confines of our home, my drinking had a devastating effect. The only thing "high" about my behavior at home was me.

While it's true I never became physically violent when drunk, I perpetrated an emotional violence upon my wife and children that was at times perhaps even more painful. Most of the time, I was withdrawn and unapproachable. When I did speak, it was to criticize harshly and to impose my rigid and unrealistic expectations on everyone else. I would humiliate my children in front of their friends. I was someone to be avoided.

I will not burden you with the ugly details of my alcoholism. Suffice it to say that for twenty years it was a horrendous burden on our family.

As I write this I am recovering from my problem. I took my last drink over 15 years ago and have since learned and practiced certain principles that have restored a healthier balance in my life. Part of my recovery has involved making amends to my family for the hardships caused by my addiction. As I have done this, we have reflected together on how we got through the worst moments with our family still intact.

How did we survive all of that? I give a great deal of the credit to my wife, who through her resilient character and deep integrity, and the strength of her love, was able to hold things together when I couldn't. My son and daughter deserve kudos as well for their ability at times to assume a maturity of perspective beyond their years. But with all due credit to their fortitude, every one of us agrees that we would not have made it without humor.

Fortunately, fun and play, wherever and whenever possible, had been endorsed and encouraged with our children from the beginning. It was permissible, therefore, to use humor to put my hurtful behavior in perspective. During family play sessions, the children were permitted to "make fun" of my aloofness and my rigid rules, and I was able to laugh along with them. This kind of interaction was a staple of our time together. As the children became more and more gifted in mimicry and satire, it did not destabilize the family relationships. It strengthened them. And it provided a sense of hope that held us together.

Another Fun Factor "ritual" that proved valuable was our

frequently played game of "tickle bug" when the children were in their early years. They never tired of it, nor did I. It was a game I could play, even when I was loaded.

Night after night I would roll on the floor laughing hysterically as the kids "attacked" me with tickling, over and over, together or in tandem. I believe that this ritual served to defuse with laughter the anger and resentment that my active alcoholism was arousing day by day. Who knows what other options the children might have chosen to express their rage, had this ritual not been available?

We are all grateful today that this kind of fun and laughter was permissible and available to us when we needed it. I am especially grateful to my parents for teaching me that there is safety and healing in laughter. Those early lessons prepared me to continue laughing with my family even in the depths of my problem.

My daughter, who is now a beautiful young mother herself, gave an apt summary of how deeply we depended on humor to get us through, when a few years into my sobriety, she quipped at a family gathering, "Do you guys ever worry that we laugh too much?" That question was never asked during my drinking years.

In the next chapter we will get into specific applications of strategies that will turn mundane family rituals into more fun for all. But there is one more general issue I would like to discuss first. It is the issue of punishment in the fun-based, fearless happy family. What happens when someone breaks the rules? How can discipline be meted out in a manner consistent with the spirit of fun we are advocating?

A family that does not tell the truth to one another compromises the possibilities for its members to be successful in the outside world. One truth that certainly must be learned by the younger members is that there are consequences to all behavior. The parents in a fun-based family must try to reward good decisions and discourage bad ones without resorting to measures that instill fear and undermine self-esteem.

The challenge is to create so much fun in the family interaction that it is punishment enough for a member to be temporarily excluded as a consequence of breaking the rules. In other words, the penalty for bad behavior becomes the withholding of something good, rather than the administering of something bad. This positive reinforcement is a more powerful influence than the negative alternatives. It fits the natural pattern of humor nature to do the right thing for the pleasure it brings, not the pain it avoids.

Once again we stress that discipline is the key to a successful, fearless happy family. True discipline celebrates the exercise of sound judgment and good decision-making. The fun-based atmosphere of such a family teaches discipline, while eliminating the fear of making mistakes. There is an emphasis on progress rather than perfection.

As we have seen in our examples, humor mitigates fear on many levels. The fear of ridicule and humiliation is diminished when laughter teaches that we are all cut out of the same imperfect mold. Mistakes become learning opportunities, not reasons for shame. The fear of corporal punishment can even be handled with humor, as illustrated by this reported experience:

My brother and I were testing Dad's patience with our bickering. Finally his limit was reached and he said, "Boys, this is your last warning. If I hear one more word, I'm taking off my belt, and you know what's going to happen then."

Brother replied, "Yeah, your pants will fall down."

Dad was laughing too hard to give us a spanking that day.

Another fear that falls by the wayside in a fun-based family is that of sharing true feelings. Humor and play provide a vehicle for expressing emotions that might otherwise be too difficult or unacceptable.

Perhaps most important of all the fears to be quelled is the fear of family dissolution or abandonment. This brings us full circle back to the first smile, which is the basis of family fun. When family life is inspired by that intimate transaction, a deep bedrock of safety and confidence nourishes the self-affirming roots of love and acceptance, out of which comes the willingness to grow and take risks. Children who are reared in such an atmosphere become adults who have no limits to their success.

Chapter Three

TRUST AND DISCIPLINE IN A FEARLESS, FUN-FILLED FAMILY

We touched briefly on the issue of discipline in the previous chapter, but I think it deserves more of our attention. In my opinion, trust and discipline are intertwined as the two most essential building blocks for a family that chooses to embrace the Fun Factor on a daily basis.

Once a private issue between parents and children, the idea of discipline in the home has lately been illuminated by public scrutiny. Concern over possible child abuse has held parents increasingly accountable for the means by which children are "disciplined." "Spare the rod and spoil the child" seems to have given way to a preoccupation with children's rights, that at times goes beyond meddlesome to frank intimidation of parents who are earnestly trying to fulfill their responsibilities. It's difficult to tell who's in charge when children retain legal counsel for the purpose of suing Mom and Pop for alleged abuses. What was once considered a parent's prerogative may now be a cause for legal action.

This contentious arena is what comes to mind most often when the term "family discipline" is mentioned. However, in this chapter I want to focus upon an entirely different aspect of discipline, namely the development of self-discipline. Whereas disciplinary action often carries a punitive connotation, self-discipline does not, unless you don't like yourself.

Sadly, self-discipline seems to be in short supply these days in America. A recent article in a national news magazine highlights an apparent trend towards rule breaking, citing a bevy of popular rationalizations. In an environment where large institutions of business and government often appear to have rendered the individual citizen powerless, the authors suggest, "... people are perversely cheating to restore fairness." (*U.S. News & World Report,* May 6, 2002, Vol. 132: No. 15, p.4)

America is already notorious throughout the world for its excesses. No other society consumes energy and goods as voraciously as ours. It is even arguable that our most challenging current health problems stem from the inability to curb our rampant self-indulgences. Our unchecked consumption may in time threaten to consume even ourselves.

How is this multi-layered social issue relevant to our discussion of the Fun Factor in a fearless family unit? What has involvement in family games during childhood got to do with resisting the adult temptations to fudge the numbers on our income tax or slip office supplies into our pockets because "the company can afford it?"

It has to do with the close connection between fun and self-discipline. We have proven time and again that we cannot legislate or enforce moderation of our ravenous appetites. Our only hope is for a national resurgence of self-discipline. This is precisely where the fearless fun-filled family unit becomes critical.

It is within the safe structure of a fun-based family that we learn the necessary early lessons that build self-esteem and self-discipline. In this sense the family that plays together, not only stays together, but also teaches its members habits of mutual respect and good discipline.

Here's how it works. Think back to that critical moment of the infant's first smile and recall how much is at stake in this early parent-child transaction. The infant is extremely vulnerable as he seeks acceptance with this rudimentary social offering. The smile is the best he can do to elicit an approving and affirming response. We can see the soil ripe for planting the first seeds of self-esteem. What will be learned from this experience?

The roots of what will eventually become self-discipline originate in the deep soil of self-esteem. If fear is the response to the infant's spontaneous expression of humor nature, then fun will always be accompanied by mistrust and probable pain. In the wake of disapproval or rejection, trusting future smiles will be more difficult. He will learn that his best is not good enough.

If the infant gets an encouraging response, then it will be safe to smile again. There is only one affirming response that counts. Anything short of a smile in return will register as a rejection. That's how delicate things are in these earliest moments of learning self-esteem. That's how powerful smiling can be before there are any words.

Let us assume that the adult in this interaction is able to momentarily set aside the fear of the awesome responsibilities looming in her new role, and instead focus on the joy of the moment. Not only has she communicated wordlessly that the infant is entirely welcome and acceptable, but also that smiling (fun) is an endorsed method of discourse. That's a lot to say silently, but it gets across. It's a message that communicates mutual trust, an absolute must for learning self-confidence. And as self-confidence sows the seeds for self-esteem in the infant, it reinforces the same attitudes in the adult.

This two-way process is important. One of the tenets of fearless family fun is that it can never be unilateral. It is either mutual or it is not at all. Unilateral fun ends up being at someone's expense and soon communicates fear.

Trust is the atmosphere for building self-confidence and self esteem, both of which lead directly to increased self-discipline. The smile teaches the infant that the world is safe and trustworthy. Withholding a smile teaches the opposite.

The smile also teaches the infant to trust himself. He need not be afraid of this early expression of his propensity for playfulness.

Without the affirming response, he learns that his most natural inclinations might lead to trouble, thus making it difficult to trust them.

I know I am making a big deal of an interaction that is rather commonplace and fleeting. But it is just this simple. If the foundation is faulty, the structure is unsafe. If a family is to thrive in a fearless, fun-filled atmosphere it is essential to build a strong foundation and that starts with the first smile.

Another piece of a strong family fun foundation is the mealtime ritual. Eating and feeding have always been an intensely social event. From very early on this becomes an opportunity for experiencing fun and play.

A moment's reflection will serve to remind us that there is a grand tradition in human history for making mealtime a happy time. The benefits for digestion alone are well documented. But more than the gustatory advantage derived from having fun while eating, a family bonding experience can come from mealtimes, provided the atmosphere is pleasant.

Let's look in on a parent-child feeding interaction sometime in the first 18 months of the child's life:

It usually looks and sounds like a game. We hear the adult in a cheerful tone of voice uttering such phrases as "Open up the tunnel; here comes the choo-choo train!" or "Vroom, vroom – the airplane is coming into the airport:" or even, "MMMH! This is good." There are likely to be bits of food spattered and scattered all about, some actually in the baby's mouth. It looks like the food fight scene from "Animal House." What is being communicated here?

The adult is telling the baby that food is good and that meals should be fun. Good start. Unfortunately, too often this scene deteriorates relatively rapidly, when, 18 months or so later, we are likely to hear the same parent sternly admonishing, "Don't play with your food!" What is a baby to think?

As children grow older and are able to feed themselves, the family meal can become a vehicle for teaching rules and regulations. If this represents a pleasant atmosphere, the learning will be fun.

But it is not just the mechanics of proper eating style that can be learned.

The family meal event is an opportunity to learn the rudiments, disciplines, and, yes, the joys involved in conversation. Too many families subscribe to the notion that "children should be seen and not heard" at mealtimes. By doing so they pass up a marvelous chance to teach self-discipline.

The give and take of conversation at the table of a fun-filled family meal must be exactly that – give and take. Having one's say is only part of the experience. Being heard is another and that comes from active listening. This occurs when all members in their turn are recipients of the family's full attention.

A favorite mealtime game in our family has long been what we call "You wanna' hear a joke?" It is usually started by one of the youngsters asking that question. Everyone listens to the joke, which is most often a riddle with a ridiculous answer. After we laugh, another member volunteers a silly one. Soon each in turn has had a chance to make one up. Of late this game has evolved into a variation on the riddle motif – "What am I?" With this game the "leader" gives a one-sentence clue, and based on that information, the other players must guess what he or she is.

It's obvious how such simple rituals teach, not only the joy of laughing together, but the discipline of waiting one's turn and the courtesy of listening to others. On the rare occasion when the joke is "offensive", it is simply discouraged while pointing out that we are already having fun without exceeding certain limits.

One family fun ritual that is easy to overlook is the saying of grace with each meal. Whether or not the family is "religious" is beside the point. The issue here is teaching the habit of gratitude. Remember that among the effective fun strategies we discussed earlier was the intention to "celebrate everything." When we put this into practice it has the effect of increasing our awareness of the things we have for which we can be truly grateful at any time.

Saying grace or giving thanks before every meal is a good example of practicing the strategy of celebration. I have been with a family who holds hands around the table and repeats the simplest of prayers, "God is great! God is good! And we thank him for our food. Amen." Then as everyone lets go of handclasps, we shout in unison, "Hallelujah!" Can you imagine how much fun that is for the kids? They actually look forward to the experience of giving thanks and ask for it if it appears to be overlooked.

As I say, this is not so much a religious indoctrination as a fun way to teach gratitude for the food we otherwise consume mindlessly at every meal. Reinforcing gratitude for those things we take for granted is fun and can curb that tendency for voracious consumption we were lamenting at the beginning of this chapter.

Still another discipline that can be taught and reinforced in the fun-filled family meal ritual is simply showing up. It becomes obvious that, in order to sustain this richly rewarding experience, there must be a set time when everyone gathers at the table. Eating on the run or at separate times will not get it done and must be discouraged. The family meal must take precedence over the many competing demands of individual schedules. This requires the commitment, and self-discipline of all. This is more likely to happen if it is viewed as a fun time to be together.

Closely related to the daily family meals, are the times, such as holidays or special events, when meals attract perhaps a more extended family gathering. Thanksgiving, religious holidays, birthdays, weddings and graduations are examples of opportunities to practice ritualistic fun. Respect for the role of tradition is taught and learned.

The Thanksgiving meal serves as an excellent example in our family of how humor and fun infiltrate the ritual if we are willing. For years we have instituted a "go around" at the Thanksgiving meal, during which everyone is asked to say what he or she is most thankful for. Everyone gets a chance, especially the children. It's a time of literally pouring out our hearts to one another. The process often takes longer than the meal. It is accompanied by much laughter, and some tears. By the time we are through it is clear that our "blessings" are more abundant than we anticipated. Even the youngest grandchild gets the point.

Another Thanksgiving memory serves as an explicit example

of how a tradition of fun can "save the day" even when unforeseen occurrences threaten to disrupt the occasion. Several years ago we were seated around the dining room table, in anticipation of our holiday feast. The family members present that day were my wife, both of her parents and our two teenaged children.

I was in the kitchen putting the finishing touches on my grand contribution to the meal, a Caesar's Salad, my crowning (and only) achievement as a culinary artist. Upon completing the preparation, I called to my 15-year-old son, Greg, asking him to help by carrying the salad into the dining room, while I fetched some utensils.

He promptly got a tray and with much pomp and ceremony carried the salad into the dining room on his shoulder, as if he were a butler, announcing in a formal voice, "Here comes the salad!"

This was amusing until, as he reached the table, the bowl full of salad slid off the back of the tray, flipped in the air, and landed face down on the carpet.

I was following close behind him and had to observe helplessly the unfolding of this "catastrophe." My son had single-handedly turned my Caesar's salad into a tossed salad with "house dressing." The room was suddenly quiet as Greg and I looked at one another. He was awaiting my response with, shall we say, heightened anticipation.

At that very moment it seemed I had a choice. I could have laughed or I could have strangled him. But there really was no choice. The whole scene, including the look on Greg's face, was so funny I had to laugh.

So I burst out laughing and, as I did, Greg assumed that he was forgiven. And he was correct, at least for the moment. I seem to recall we discussed it later, but that's another story.

The important point is that the laughter freed us all to go on with our enjoyment of the occasion. Even my father-in-law smiled as he carefully picked an anchovy off one of his spotlessly shined shoes.

Thus, over time, everyday meals supplemented by special occasion meals become fundamental events in the enjoyment of fun-filled family interaction. Once a strong foundation is laid down, the family becomes free to infuse many activities with fun, which will further serve to reinforce the self-esteem and ultimately the self-discipline of all members.

A frequent venue for family fun is an outdoor excursion. This can take many forms, from a few minutes of play in the backyard to taking a walk together, or having a picnic in the local park. Simple games such as hide and seek or tag can eventually evolve to more structured fun such as badminton, croquet or horseshoes. Such precedence for spontaneous outdoor activity provides a powerful attraction as time goes on to keep the family close.

A busy and successful surgeon, his wife, a registered nurse, and their two sons, ages 17 and 14, were recently interviewed. Their enjoyment of one another was obvious as they talked in the kitchen of their home. They agreed that a strong commitment to full participation in outdoor activity had kept their family fun alive and strong, despite the busy careers of both parents.

When the boys were small, family excursions were taken on tandem bicycles so that all could be included. Today, all four participate in several cycling events each year and have cycled together through Yellowstone National Park, the Grand Tetons and even Switzerland.

And how do the teenagers feel about being a part of such a closely-knit family? The oldest says, "Among my friends, at least half their parents are divorced. They have to go back and forth between houses and worst of all they end up liking one parent more than the other. That's horrible. That should never happen." His younger brother adds, "Kids want to hang out with our family because we do fun things." (*Kentuckiana Health/Fitness Magazine*, Vol. 5: #10, April, 2002, p. 18)

Perhaps the most "famous" example of ritualistic outdoor family fun in recent memory is the frequency of touch football games at the much-publicized gatherings of the Kennedy clan. These highly spirited intra-family contests were known to break out with great regularity, sometimes even on the grounds of the White House.

Which brings us to a generalization about effective family fun. The universal ingredient in all our examples of family play is the ability of all members to be present and focused on the same activity. Even in instances where a family member's active participation is not possible, it is important for the member be physically present to "participate" in the spirit of the fun. The spirit of personal participation is even more important than the participation itself.

To reiterate, the activity in question need not be confined to a game or some other form of ritualized play. Many things fall into the category of fearless family fun, even though they might never provoke a laugh. Just looking at a sunset together or listening to music can be fun without requiring an outburst of playful repartee. Again, the critical common denominator is that the activity is done together, with the full participation of all members. No one is excluded or exempt.

In my experience it is usually one of the parents who allows a distraction to interfere. Every potential distraction should be challenged lest the message be sent that family fun is a relatively trivial pursuit (not to be confused with the game of the same name). The right message is especially critical to the growing self-esteem and self-discipline of the children.

This brings up the instances of family members encouraging and supporting one another in individual pursuits. This frequently takes the form of parental enthusiasm for a child's involvement in "extracurricular activities" at school or in the community, such as sports, music or other forms of self-expression. The personal involvement of an adult to help structure and promote a child's development in these kinds of undertakings provides enhanced discipline and motivation for which the child may be very grateful later in life. Many a successful entertainer has a persistent "stage mom" to thank.

Consequently, parental attendance at events such as games

or performances is an important expression of personal endorsement and is to be encouraged. It obviously has a beneficial effect on self-esteem. But this is not what we are talking about in this chapter. Family fun is not a spectator sport. It calls for full participation. In this sense, playing a game amongst family members is of more potential value than going to watch one of the kids play a Little League game, though both are important.

Of course when weather does not permit outdoor activity, indoor games provide the family with many alternatives. From Candy Land to Monopoly and beyond, board games are excellent vehicles for teaching the enjoyment that can be had from following the rules. These games give youngsters the opportunity to treat parents more like peers and vice versa. Another important benefit is that most games encourage conversation amongst the participants, thus equating effective communication with an enjoyable experience.

A favorite indoor activity for many families is family show time. This usually involves the children putting on a performance for the adults. In our family, show time was quite a production. The children would seat the parents in the "theatre" (often the playroom or living room). Then we would be treated to a lavish production that could be anything from a gymnastics exhibition to a scene from a favorite movie, or a satire on a recent family event. Re-enacting the television program, Masterpiece Theatre, was a frequent and popular theme when our kids were small.

What these productions lacked in polish was more than made up for in zest and originality. Not only would we laugh and applaud, but, in the bargain, we were from time to time likely to receive keen insights into how our parenting skills looked from the other side of the fence. Children can be embarrassingly accurate in their mimicry.

We turn now to the world's most relationship-intensive activity—the family trip. With the possible exception of the occasional crowded elevator, there is no other experience in life that compares with the face-to-face enforced intimacy of a long trip in the family car, or for that matter on a plane. The only difference is that, with air travel, there are usually witnesses who don't belong to the family. So you can't be as spontaneous.

It is in the experience of the family car trip that the greatest opportunities arise to teach and learn important lessons in patience and self-discipline. As in every example we've discussed, there is the choice between fear and fun as a means of maintaining decorum. Perhaps a recollection from my own family will illustrate the potential for choosing fun.

Our family's first objective for every vacation trip I can ever recall was to get an early start. It didn't matter to my Dad how far we were going. It only mattered that we beat the traffic there. Consequently, the car had to be packed the day before. I say the day before, because evening would have been long past the vacation eve curfew. You see, on the day before our planned departure, we all went to bed shortly after lunch, so we could be awakened for our early start the next morning.

Memories of packing the car bring to mind the second major objective for our family vacation. As stated by my Dad it was always "to get away from it all." I never really understood this because to me it always looked like we were taking "it all" with us. We brought along everything that wasn't nailed down.

We packed 10 suitcases for four people for five days. Every nook and cranny of the car was filled with something, with additional "necessities" lashed to the roof. *Grapes of Wrath* had nothing on us. By the time the car was packed the house was empty. We never had a problem with break-ins while we were gone. There was nothing left behind to steal.

My mother would even bring along our winter coats ... to the seashore ... in August. This always drove Dad over the brink. "Good grief Betty, why the winter coats in the middle of August?" She would always answer him the same way. "First of all," she would start off slowly, " my name is Doris! And second, it might get chilly at the shore in the evenings."

So, now let us fast-forward to the moment of our pre-dawn departure. My brother and I would be packed half asleep into the back seat, buried somewhere under the coats. Dad was driving and Mom was, of course, riding shotgun. By the time we were four blocks from home, our muffled voices could be heard asking the universal kids' question—"Are we there yet?" It is a question all children are obliged to ask incessantly on every trip longer than the length of their driveways.

"Are we there yet? Are we there yet? When are we going to get there?"

I don't know about your dad, but I can tell you ours was a master at evading this question. He did so by answering in riddles that would have confused the Oracle of Delphi. His first answer to the question, "Are we there yet?" was always this little puzzler: "Relax boys, we'll be there in no time at all."

No time at all! Was ever such a thing possible? How do we get from Point A to Point B without any time elapsing? If we could, wouldn't we be constantly doing it? As long as we stayed on the move, we'd never age. We'd be eternally youthful. Come on. There's only one human being in all of history who's been able to accomplish that feat—Dick Clark. And he's not divulging his secrets.

So Dad's first answer would never do the trick. We would see through to the logical fallacy and resume our interrogation.

"Are we there yet?"

But Dad had an even better answer in reserve. It was an answer that would simultaneously confuse us and strike terror in our hearts. He would summon his most reassuring tone and announce. "Be patient. We're going to be there before you know it."

Now that sounds reassuring until the words begin to sink in. Think about it. Do you really ever want to arrive somewhere before you know it? At the very least, I think that would be more than a little embarrassing. People might ask, "Say, when did you get here?" Then you'd have to say, "Gee, I don't know. Am I here yet?"

Besides, what's the point of being there if you don't know it? You wouldn't have the presence of mind to grab the good seats. Who knows what will be available by the time you realize you're there. Plus, you might leave before you arrive and meet yourself coming and going.

No, thank you. I prefer to know it precisely when I arrive, not before or after. I don't mind telling you that Dad's answer would have been enough to make me stop asking altogether and surrender to my impending suffocation under the coats, had not Mom jumped in to save the day. Her suggestion was simple but at the same time profound. She merely tried to demonstrate that it was not necessary to wait until we arrived at our destination to have fun. She believed we could have a good time on the way as well.

Her first idea was always for everyone to sing together. If your Mom was anything like mine, you already know what kinds of songs she wanted us to sing. The problem with "On Top of Old Smokey" and "The Battle Hymn of the Republic" was that we only knew the dirty words that we had learned from the older kids in the back of the school bus. When my brother and I held forth with our lyrics, the singing portion of our trip would come to an abrupt and premature end.

Next she would suggest, "Why don't you boys count license plates or look for farm animals?" Clearly she was teaching us that there is as much fun in the travel as there is at the destination. To her, "Are we there yet?" was the wrong question. "Are we having fun yet?" was more to the point. How profound.

I only wish I had learned her lesson well back then. After many years of chasing remote goals while overlooking the beauty of each present moment, I finally realized the wisdom it contained. Belatedly I learned to stop asking, "Am I there yet?" and ask the more useful question, "Am I having fun?" But it didn't have to take me as long as it did. The lessons had been there all along in the play opportunities offered on our family trips.

Once everyone is distracted from the 'wrong question," there are many fun-filled options to fill the hours spent on the road. We are not talking here about a diversion. I know that some families currently have the means to "keep the kids entertained" with a movie on the car's VCR. But this is not nearly as beneficial as a word game that involves everyone.

Rhyming was a popular en route game in our car. In this simple game, one member says a word and it is up to the others to think of words that rhyme with it. The winner is the one who has the last word, after which nobody can think of any more. The winner's prize is the privilege of starting the next round with a word of his or her choosing.

"Collecting" license plates is another game that everyone gets to play. All it requires is daylight and a reasonable amount of traffic. Due to my dad's early start policy, our family had to wait several hours, at least until sunrise, before we could play this one. Each member collects a list of license plates they spot from various states. The one who spots it first gets to write it down. In cases of a tie, both get credit. Of course the winner is the one who collects the longest list.

When all else fails, the family can always resort to sightseeing, or "view time," as it is often called. Although this is sometimes unpopular with the kids at the time, it provides many memories that are fun to rehash as time goes on. Dad pulls over at a designated "Scenic Overlook" and orders everybody out of the car to stand together to admire the view. After paying appropriate "homage" to whatever the sight, everyone piles back into the car refreshed for having broken the monotony.

I want to end this chapter by discussing the issue of trust. By now we have seen how the fun-filled fearless family is built on trust. That trust is what builds self-confidence and self-esteem. Clearly, when these two values are high, self-discipline becomes more likely and effective.

It is easiest to see how trust is critical for the developing children in the family. If trust is betrayed, they are extremely vulnerable. Playfulness is a way of reaching out with the best they have. If their natural expression of fun is not supported and acceptable, they have no other options than to adopt defensive and fear-based personal habits designed to limit pain and rejection. Normal development requires a trustworthy family culture.

It is more difficult to recognize that the need for trust is equally critical on the part of the adults involved. As we pointed out, the parents have a choice. They can endorse fun and encourage it, or they can react more sternly and authoritatively out of fear. Choosing fun requires trust on many levels.

First there must be trust in one's own sense of humor, or as we have named it, humor nature. We must respect that quiet voice within that urges us to have fun against all our "puritanical" inhibitions. We must be willing to let others see the childlike, sometimes mischievous, elements of our character. In other words we must have confidence in our basic trustworthiness. We must hold ourselves in sufficiently high esteem. For some this is difficult because the self-esteem issue was not adequately addressed in their own early family experiences. The omissions of one generation become the limitations of the next.

Second, parents must trust humor and fun to get the job done. This kind of trust is not easy to come by in a social atmosphere that too often equates responsibility with seriousness. The notion that humor is "trustworthy" comes in part from the testimony of others and the growing body of research that confirms its benefits. But there is really no substitute for personal experience over time. The willingness to rely more and more on humor nature, even when facing serious challenges, is the chief strategy for overcoming doubts. When we do this we are greatly encouraged.

Finally, after trusting their motives and the method, parents must trust the other members of the family, principally the children. There is always the fear that endorsing fun will encourage youngsters to exploit the situation to the detriment of all. As we have mentioned, this concern is rarely justified; yet it persists.

So we see that trust is a necessity for family fun. I hope that some of the examples cited in this chapter will encourage more willingness to take the risk. There is no one tradition or "game" that is better than any other. Each family must find the activities that best fit its style. It will help to remember that, as we see in all the vignettes, it is of paramount importance to focus more on the opportunity for family members to enjoy each other, than on the game or ritual itself. When the focus is on the game more than the people involved, we have already missed the point.

Chapter Four

REWARDING AND REINFORCING THE FUN FACTOR
IN THE FAMILY

There is more to be gained from life in a fearless, fun-filled family than the development of self-esteem and self-discipline, as important and fundamental as those issues might be. All of the families highlighted in the previous chapters could be described as functional, to be sure. Notice the word functional contains the word fun. I do not think that is a coincidence. We have illustrated how fun energizes and inspires the rituals of the fearless family. Indeed, where families are concerned, fun-filled is synonymous with functional.

This being true, the opposite is also worth noting. The hallmark of a dysfunctional family is the absence of humor and fun in its everyday life. Again, it's no coincidence that the term dysfunctional contains the word dysfun. In medical parlance the prefix "dys" means bad, impaired, painful or difficult. Impaired or painful aptly describes the "fun" within a dysfunctional family. There is far too much threat and counter-threat in the air, which makes mutual trust virtually impossible.

A dysfunctional family doesn't play. The absence of play in common parlance means rigidity or lack of flexibility. When we say, "There is no play in the line," we mean it is too taut or tense. So it is in the fear-based dysfunctional family. There is no tolerance for the mutual vulnerability of play amongst its members.

In contrast, the fun-filled family has a margin for error. Mistakes are not only tolerated, but can be positive learning opportunities. It is the difference between teaching either perfection or perfectionism. As we learned earlier, the first is fun; the second is fearful.

All of which results in the fearlessness we have described in the fun-filled family interactions. Whereas fear is without fun, fun is fearless.

In the last chapter we gave examples of the many ways families can practice playfulness. We illustrated the most common opportunities to encourage fun and teach its principles. In this chapter we will explore the values and characteristics that are demonstrated by fun-filled family members as they extend themselves to one another and beyond the family.

As we noted before, these values are communicated from parents to children more by behavior than words. Children are watching every move and learning more from what parents practice than from what they preach. "Do as I say, not as I do," will not work in the fearless family. Parents must walk their talk. They must be participators in the family games, or their endorsements of fun ring hollow.

What follows is a partial list of the values that get transmitted and adopted through the daily "rituals" of a fun-based family. Each is more likely to be communicated implicitly than explicitly. We start with the first, and perhaps most important, value taught in fun-filled family life.

The Value of Integrity

All family games have rules. As children learn to play by the rules they are laying down a foundation for personal integrity. This developmental task is made less onerous in the fun-filled family, as it becomes clear that in every game there is more fun to be had by following the rules than by breaking them.

Yet, there is a deeper, subtler, level of integrity observable in the fearless family. Parents who, not only indulge play, but also are willing to participate in it, will communicate this valuable trait silently. Following the examples of their playful parents, children soon learn to back up words with consistent action. They see that it is important to say what you mean and mean what you say. Over time they realize commitment is important and that it requires being there and being involved.

Jim, a recovering cancer patient, showed up for his support group one afternoon sporting purple hair. Everyone feared that he perhaps had fallen prey to a weird and belated "side effect" from his chemotherapy. He was quick to reassure us.

"It's kind of embarrassing, but it's nothing serious," he announced. "I simply lost a bet."

He explained that he had made a deal with his 15-year-old daughter. Both claiming to be the best "Scrabble" players in the family, they challenged one another to a "winner take all" match up. She had agreed that if he won, she would give up her "punk" look and get a "normal" haircut. In return, if she was able to beat him, he agreed to dye his hair whatever color she chose.

Guess who won.

"She told me I didn't really have to go through with it, but fair is fair," he chuckled. "I certainly would have held her to the deal, if I had won."

"Anyway," he added, "it'll all grow out in a few weeks."

As life goes on, the intention to be "as good as one's word" is a valuable asset to success. Dependability, reliability and integrity open doors of opportunity and elicit cooperation from others. The adult whose childhood has been filled with repeated examples of this behavior is likely to perpetuate it and encourage others to do the same.

The Value of Facing the Truth

This value is closely related to the first one. It too is learned more by absorption than articulation. It involves the capacity to be comfortable with the truth. When a family allows humor to prevail, it becomes easier for each member to accept what is true.

Humor nature reflects the truth. That is why there is no humor in the dysfunctional family. There are just too many lies that must be "protected."

The truth is that, as humor beings, we are all connected, like Siamese twins, at the heart. Our differences are nothing more than superficial figments of imagination, maintained by the fear of losing so-called individuality. We become reacquainted with this truth every time we face a life-threatening event, such as a war or a natural disaster. At those moments we always say the same thing: "United we stand; divided we fall. Why can't we live this way all the time?"

Never are we closer to the truth about our connectedness than when we are sharing fun and laughter. The fearless fun-filled family devotes every day to celebration and perpetuation of this healthy unity. Its members learn to "live this way all the time."

It is also true that we make frequent mistakes and that, inevitably, there are consequences from every action we take. Such truths can be difficult to accept in an atmosphere of rigidity and fear. Fun embraces these realities and teaches us how to live with them. By facing the truth fearlessly when failure occurs, the fun-filled family commits its energy to growth and adaptation, not guilt and shame. This crosses generational lines to benefit all members, children and adults.

Recently, I invited my son to accompany me to a speaking engagement, only to have him witness firsthand one of the worst "performances" I have ever given. No matter what I tried that evening, the audience wasn't buying it. Gaining their undivided attention was like herding cats, and I failed miserably.

As I struggled to the end of my ordeal, it was painfully clear that, as a speaker, I had made no discernable impact on anyone.

Dragging my battered ego off the dais, I was embarrassed and ashamed.

"I'm sorry you had to see that," I told my son dejectedly. He hugged me and whispered, "Whatever you do, keep smiling." After shaking a few hands and thanking our hostess, we retired to a quiet corner of the hotel's coffee shop.

My son seized the initiative.

"Before you say anything, I want you to hear this," he said in measured tones. "That speech is probably the worst public flop I've ever seen you commit. But it pales in comparison to some of the stupid things you've done over the years and we've already had some laughs about them. If my respect for you depended on you getting it right all the time, I would have lost it long ago. I want you to know that, if anything, after watching you tonight, I have even more respect and love for you than before."

By the time we left the hotel, we were both laughing like little children as we recalled some of the silly and stupid episodes in our family's history. When family members can help each other face the truth with positive perspective, there is no such thing as failure.

The Value of Simplicity

Einstein once wrote, "Everything should be made as simple as possible; but no simpler." Keeping things simple in life is a daily challenge.

First, there is our tendency to confuse simple with easy. They are not the same thing. T.S. Eliot writes, " Simplicity is difficult because it requires nothing less than absolutely everything." Simple is not easy; but neither is it complicated.

Second, just remembering to do the simplest thing at any time is a challenge to our self-discipline. For example, try smiling constantly for the next two hours. Chances are you won't be able to do it. Yet, a smile is the simplest of behaviors, totally under your control. The failure will be in remembering to keep it going. Smiling is simple, but remembering to do it is not easy.

As we've discovered, family fun begins with a simple, but

profound smile. Nowhere is the power of simplicity more evident than in that first infant-parent transaction. Subsequent success in creating and maintaining a fearless, fun-filled family atmosphere requires close adherence to the spirit of that simple moment. That's why the essence of functional family play is action, not words. When interactions are kept that simple, spontaneity and freedom of expression are enhanced.

With fun, the fewer words, the better. Children raised in a fun-based family grow to understand that play can be an effective shorthand for communicating complicated information, sometimes obviating the necessity for overly long and difficult discussions.

The Value of Communication

Few skills are more valued in the fun-filled family than those that enhance communication. The generalization that healthy family play is most often group-oriented, not solitary, speaks to the potential power it has to reinforce competent self-expression. Also, the endorsement of humor and fun as a reliable and respectful mode of discourse encourages a full range of expressiveness.

Verbalization is the medium we most often focus upon when assessing communication effectiveness. Yet we know from research that the spoken word usually accounts for less than 10 percent of the information we are transmitting. Emotional tone, facial expression, body posture and timing are among the more efficient expressive tools. Family play is a veritable "laboratory" for the testing and proving of these many facets.

Games and rituals enhance the non-verbal aspects of self-expression. Pure expressions of the joy of interacting do not need words to expand or explain them. The thrill and satisfaction that comes from being included is self-evident. The energy of fun communicates on a level that is often too deep for words, its roots dating back to that first (preverbal) smile.

But expression is at the most only half the value of communication. Family games offer templates upon which members learn the value of paying attention to one another.

A family game of whisper-down-the-lane can produce more

laughter and fun than a circus full of clowns. It is impossible to predict what the word will sound like when it gets to the end of the line, but you can be sure it will bear no discernable relationship to the original.

A participant in a Fun Factor workshop reported a "marathon" game played at a Labor Day gathering of four families, fifteen people in all. He recalled that the word "frequency" was transformed into "sing off key", while "California" became "false menus."

The seemingly passive act of paying close attention is in reality another form of expression. When each member "gets a turn" in a family game, the others, by sharing the spotlight, are saying, "You are important." Fun-filled family rituals reinforce the value of paying attention, another essential ingredient of success in life.

The Value of Listening
The value of listening carefully is closely related to that of paying attention. As above, what seems like a passive state is anything but passive. Reception is an active task. Seeking to understand is the greatest honor one family member can bestow on another.

Life in the fun-filled family soon teaches that the successful expression of humor nature depends upon careful listening. Professional comedians verify that, even when it comes to the performance aspects of humor, listening, not speaking, is the most essential skill. So it is in the functional family. Members not only pay attention, but also seek to understand one another.

This is best illustrated by the ritual of 'inside jokes", a common phenomenon in many fearless families. To participate in the inside joke, each member must be paying attention. In addition, he must be listening for subtle cues, which would go unnoticed by outsiders.

Fran, a breast cancer survivor, told her support group about an inside joke that occurred with her family shortly after her mastectomy.

The patient, her two teenaged daughters and her husband decided to go out for dinner. It so happened that it was Fran's first social outing with the family since her discharge from the hospital.

When it was Fran's turn to order from the menu, she asked the waitress, "How good is your chicken special?"

"Delicious," was the answer. "We have breasts, thighs and drumsticks and you get to choose two pieces in any combination."

"I'll take it," decided Fran. Then looking mischievously at both of her daughters, she added, " And, I'd like two breasts, please."

The entire family burst out laughing, and the waitress is probably still wondering to this day what was so funny.

The Courage to Try New Things

No one denies that courage has value. Often we attribute this value to dramatically heroic acts of valor, during a crisis. Most people who exhibit that level of courage will confess that in the heat of the moment they simply did what they had to do. They didn't really have time to think or choose.

I am impressed with less spectacular displays of courage such as the willingness to take small risks every day, when it would appear there is time to think and choose not to act.

Growing up in a fun-filled family unit can only increase one's courage to grow and expand one's horizons. Play is the most painless way we know to learn how to take risks. When laughter can be trusted as supportive, not derisive, then "failures" can be put in perspective with humor. A mistake becomes just one more surprise. Having less to lose builds courage.

The Value of Taking Oneself Less Seriously

Most people will readily agree that there are many benefits for health and success that can come from taking one's self less seriously. However, what most often gets in the way of this strategy is the common fear that laughing at one's self risks losing the respect and confidence of others. This is not a problem in the fearless fun-filled family.

A chronic pain patient named Danny told me the following story about a deep insight he received from a family play ritual in his home. When Danny's two sons were 4 and 6 years old, one of their favorite games was Dinosaur Hunt.

The game was played like this: The boys would always be the cavemen hunting the dinosaur. The role of the dinosaur was always assigned to Danny.

One evening, after a particularly vigorous game, Danny was reflecting on it with his wife.

"Why do you think the boys never choose to be the dinosaur?" He asked her. "You'd think they'd want to be the bigger animal sometimes. Yet, no matter how ferocious I pretend to be, it never seems to frighten them to be smaller."

She thought for a moment. "Maybe they don't feel threatened because they are beginning to understand that dinosaurs eventually eliminated themselves by getting too big for their own good," she replied.

Both parents agreed that, whether or not the boys had consciously reached that level of insight, their dinosaur game held a meaningful message for any adult willing to pay attention.

As parents are willing to take themselves less seriously, children learn that such behavior is completely compatible with meeting the responsibilities involved in running the home and making critical decisions. When laughter is mutual, as in laughing with, not at, one another, youngsters learn to connect fun with compassion, understanding and support, not shame, humiliation and derision. This makes it safer to laugh at themselves.

Over time, the fun-filled family teaches its members that laughing at one's self is a sign of personal strength and a marvelous prelude to learning from mistakes.

The Value of Presence

Here is another example of a value that is difficult to put into words, but is powerfully taught when acted out. We pointed out how important it is for everyone (especially the adults) in a fun-filled family to place a high priority on showing up. The spirit of fun is compromised by absences that could have been avoided.

Fun can't be phoned in. It can't be postponed or videotaped. You have to be there or you miss out. If a family member misses out on too many opportunities to play, it sets up stratification between the "haves" and the "have-nots" – the in-group and the out-group. This limits the fun.

Keeping priorities straight is a big part of achieving presence in any activity. Family fun is a great way to learn this valuable lesson.

The Value of Surprises

How many times do we rigidly resist the unexpected in life, fearing that it can only have negative consequences? "I don't want any surprises," is the battle cry of many a busy executive about to launch a new product or implement a new corporate strategy. Is a surprise really that treacherous?

At times it would appear that the fun-filled fearless family is obsessed with surprises. This is because they have discovered that the unexpected can often be the most fun of all. What a precious insight.

One week before her birthday, we had managed to get my wife, Connie, to our daughter's house without tipping her off that a surprise birthday celebration was in the works. Everyone was carrying off the charade like professional poker players.

Things went smoothly until we sat down to dinner. Noah, who was four years old, calmly advised his grandmother, "Save room for dessert. We're having birthday cake."

"Really?" answered Connie. "Whose birthday is it?"

Noah whispered, "That's a secret!"

Children raised in a fun-filled atmosphere learn that surprising someone is fun for them, as well as for the recipient. They see that there is nothing to fear from the unexpected and that surprises are delightful gifts we give to one another.

The Value of Focus

The value of focus is very closely related to the value of

presence. Again, we are talking about the need in life to be clear about one's priorities. The country song lyric tells us, "you've got to stand for something or you'll fall for anything." How true.

As we have seen, playing games in a fearless family atmosphere teaches discipline in "following the rules." The rules serve as guiding principles that apply without exception to every circumstance that can arise during play. By practicing this discipline, children in the family learn that all decisions are guided by certain principles, which can at times override the immediate demands of any situation. This realization generalizes to life outside the family.

The capacity to keep one's priorities and values clearly in focus, regardless of circumstance, provides a compass by which to navigate through the more chaotic moments of life.

The Value of Humility

Arrogance is a major cause of suffering in life. Whenever we fall into the mistaken assumption that we are the center of the universe, we are headed for a painful disillusionment. Among other things, arrogance robs us of gratitude and perspective. It effectively prevents us from laughing at ourselves. It undermines our resilience.

An arrogant attitude does not get far in a fearless, fun-filled family. When humor prevails, it quickly and effectively punctures the puffed up ideas we tend to nurture about our own self-importance. Shared laughter is a great equalizer.

One evening, as a guest on a radio call-in show, I was taking calls on the subject of stress. I was surprised to hear my daughter's voice on one of the calls. She was a high school student at the time and had called on the air to ask my advice in handling the high level of anxiety she was feeling at exam time.

I acknowledged her as my daughter, and then, attempting to counteract the impression that I was so unapproachable as a father that she had to call a radio show to talk to me, I reminded her that she and I had discussed this very problem a few nights earlier.

"Did you try any of the suggestions I gave you over the weekend?" I asked her.

"Yes I did, Dad," she answered, "and none of them worked."

When I arrived home later that evening, she had a big smile on her face that said, "Gotcha!" loud and clear. The smirks on everyone else's faces indicated that she had been part of a family-wide prank designed to puncture my pomposity.

Humility is not evidence of weakness or timidity. It is merely the absence of arrogance, the realization of one's true place in the grand scheme of things. When we try to be humble on our own, chances are we will simply discover yet another way to be self-centered. True humility benefits from the assistance of others.

The Value of Intuition

Intuition is the source of a baby's first smile. There is no apparent calculation involved. When that fledgling smile is welcomed and returned, over and over, in a fun-based atmosphere, the infant comes to regard his intuition as reliable and trustworthy. He is likely to listen more readily to the still small voice of his humor nature as time goes on.

Soon he is invited to join in the fun of family play, during which he witnesses parents and siblings trusting their humor instincts to great effect. As he gains confidence in his own sense of humor, he expresses it more spontaneously, to the delight and approval of the others. The small voice becomes a reliable guide to fun.

At a support group meeting for cancer patients, Rachel and Allen recalled that when their oldest son was about two years old, they enjoyed a family "game" called "Baby Jokes." They would invite him to tell them a baby joke. Having no words yet, he would respond by just making voice sounds in the rhythm of a joke. When he paused at the end of his "sentence," that would be their cue to laugh. It gave him such pleasure to "make" them laugh, that his squeals of delight would eclipse their own.

Later in life the children in fun-filled families become adults who are more likely to avoid the folly of trying to please others, choosing instead to resort to their "inner guides" for feedback and self-discipline.

The Value of Graciousness in Winning and Losing

It is easy to see how all of these values are very closely connected and actually reinforce one another. This value comes out of the fun-filled family's tendency to focus more on the process of fun than its outcome. It teaches family members that the joy of mutual interaction is more important than the final score of any game.

Thus the child growing up in the fearless family learns that winning is only part of the fun, and not always the most important part. He learns to be a gracious and generous winner, grateful for the participation of his playmates. When he is on the losing side, he is able to see it in proper perspective and generously extend good feelings toward the winner(s).

It was Christmas Eve and the entire family had gathered at our son's home for dinner. The tree was trimmed and presents were carefully placed around it, making sure there was plenty of room left for Santa to add to the bounty later that night.

Our daughter, Rebecca, had knitted a sweater for Jordan, our son's oldest boy, and, since she would not be there the next morning, she wondered if he could be allowed to open that one gift on Christmas Eve, so she could see how it fit him.

Of course, Jordan was all for it, as any 5-year-old child would be. He tore into the package with gusto, reached into the box and pulled out … a sweater. Tossing the sweater behind him, he dove back in. Perhaps that was just the packing material.

As he came up empty-handed, a look of disappointment began to shroud his face. My son, anticipating an embarrassing moment, spoke up.

"Jordan, Aunt Rebecca took a long time to make you that sweater. I'm sure you'll want to thank her."

Very resolutely, Jordan picked up the sweater, walked over to Rebecca, and said in measured tones, "Aunt Rebecca, thank you for the sweater."

He smiled before continuing. "But, for my birthday, maybe you could give me a toy."

Rarely have I seen such grace under fire.

The Value of Optimism and Hope

Sharing laughter is an effective way to share hope. Whenever we laugh together we wordlessly participate in the recognition that, after all is said and done, we are all in the same boat, vulnerable to the same things. Far from a discouraging recollection, this truth is cause for optimism.

Looking at those around us, we are tempted to think that the grass is truly "greener" in the neighbor's field. As we absorb the inevitable setbacks and traumas that life doles out, it often seems that we are alone in our pain. Others do not appear to suffer as we do. These speculations lead to a sense of isolation and resentment.

However, when we see and hear those same others laughing with us, we know they wouldn't be laughing unless they recognized the same predicaments in their own experiences. The laughter tells us they have been where we are and can identify with our pain. We are relieved. It's not so much that misery loves company. It just feels good to be back in the fold.

The fearless fun-filled family recapitulates this reassuring interaction daily. The humor inherent in its playful rituals, not only makes the moment fun, but also illustrates shared vulnerabilities. When children experience parents sharing laughter with them, they learn that adults can understand fear and helplessness, because they feel it as well.

Family fun does more than communicate shared vulnerabilities. Laughter also teaches that what is painful now may, in time, be less so, if not a blessing in disguise. Humor is the best way to rekindle that hope for a pony in every pile of manure (recall Fun Commandment Ten—always look for the pony). When fun is the motivating energy in family life there is no room for hopelessness and despair.

The Value of Tradition

From the easily identified holiday rituals to the unarticulated commitment to daily routine, every family is a hotbed of tradition.

The role tradition plays is clear. By "institutionalizing" and thus perpetuating certain patterns of behavior, tradition lends predictability to family life. At the same time, tradition demands loyalty to the way things are done.

In a dysfunctional family, traditions are fear-based and painful. Loyalty is achieved through intimidation and coercion. Tyranny reigns.

In a functional, fearless family, traditions are fun. They are a means of perpetuating the joy of belonging and being together. Loyalty is freely given, based on the desire to rekindle that joy at every opportunity. Celebration reigns.

Think back to the example in the previous chapter of the family who shouted "Hallelujah!" as they gave thanks before every meal. In that family, whenever the adults were distracted and overlooked the saying of grace, the children asked for it. Why? Because it was so much fun to shout "Hallelujah!"

In fun-filled families the tradition of playfulness energizes every ritual. Members are drawn spontaneously toward every opportunity to be together. There is no stronger tradition than this.

Fred, an orthopedic surgeon, shared a recollection of a family tradition that was great fun for him and his siblings. Every year, during the Christmas season, Fred's father went all out to decorate their house and lawn with lights.

This "family project" would begin each Halloween and culminate in mid-December, the centerpiece being a life sized manger scene, designed and constructed by Fred's dad. The nativity made for an impressive display, but the most memorable thing about it was that, in addition to Mary, Joseph, baby Jesus, the shepherds and the wise men, the scene always included Rudolph the Red-Nosed Reindeer and Frosty the Snowman.

Fred said it was a shock to learn, as he grew older, that Frosty was probably not present at that first Christmas.

The Value of Resilience
Yet another largely unspoken "given" in the fearless fun-

based family, is permission to laugh and have fun as a means of reducing stress. When this is well established and understood it can provide relief at the most unpredictable times.

The support that is characteristic of family fun rituals sustains hope and bolsters morale during any crisis. Research data confirm that when we can laugh at our challenges we can more effectively meet and overcome them.

A good deal of personal resilience is related to the ability to keep a balanced perspective. As we have already observed, the family that plays together reinforces the "big picture."

The Value of Perspective

There is nothing worse in life than losing one's perspective. The best antidote for this derailment of perception is repeated exposure to the Fun Factor, especially in early family interaction.

Charlie Chaplin had it right when he said, "Life is tragedy in close-up, but comedy in long shot." The effect of fun-filled family interaction is to keep the "long shot" perspective uppermost in view.

Fun and play demonstrate the power of humor to alter our perspective. Disagreements become less problematic when fun reemphasizes common factors. In playful interaction we can recognize that individual differences are far outweighed by shared goals and values.

When he was five years old our son, Greg, had some trouble with night terrors. A night-light and some patient reassurance were usually enough to get him through a typical episode. Occasionally, when the fears refused to be quieted, his mother or I would sit with him while he fell asleep. He seemed to draw comfort from hearing us say, "Now, close your eyes, and don't open them until you're asleep."

One evening I had invited a friend over to watch Monday Night Football with me. Barely had the game begun when Greg called out. I went to his room and calmly gave him my usual reassurances. I think he sensed I was anxious to get back to the game. I left his door ajar, so he could hear us watching the game.

Two minutes later, he called again. Once more, I went to him and offered reassurance. There was an impatient edge to my words. I urged him to try his best to get to sleep. He said he would.

After another two minutes, he called a third time. I went to him again. Since my wife wasn't home, I knew that, if he didn't get it together, I was going to have to sit with him and miss more of the game. So, I told him I wanted this to be my last visit. "If I have to come to your room again, I'll be angry," I warned.

"OK," he whimpered, "but I just wish I had a father who remembered what it was like to be 5 years old."

The result was instant perspective. I never saw the first half of that football game, and I never missed it.

A perspective shift would be a challenging concept to verbalize to young children. Yet it is effectively and simply communicated without words through the spirit of fearless play.

The Value of Forgiveness

Forgiveness is commonly considered to be an act of charity, often inspired by a religious belief. As such, it is usually associated with a pious and condescending attitude that can be demeaning to the recipient. The forgiver is afforded a semblance of superiority. This is an unfortunate misrepresentation of this valuable transaction.

True forgiveness is simply the act of letting go. As such it "levels the playing field" and tears up the scorecards. It frees up both the forgiver and the forgiven. It is a common staple of fearless family play.

Think back to the Thanksgiving Caesar Salad incident from the last chapter. This is an excellent example of how forgiveness works through laughter in a fun-based family. By letting go, the family preserved its unity and the energy to proceed. In a family committed to fun, even when confrontation of undesirable behavior must occur, it can be done in a spirit of support, not rejection.

Lingering over resentments and "unresolved issues" is the chief impediment to progress in life and a major cause of human failure. Those raised in a fun-filled family know how to avoid that pitfall.

The Value of Creativity
When the fun-filled family is at play, creativity is encouraged at many levels. Any interaction based on fun and endorsing laughter lowers the inhibitions and stimulates spontaneity. Riddles and other word games are obvious examples.

George, an attendee at a recent workshop, reported a game that was very popular in his fun-filled family. He called it The Progressive Story Game.

One person would begin a story, using just one sentence – "Once upon a time, there was a king who couldn't sleep at night." The next person had to add to the story, but was also confined to one sentence. In turn, everyone had a chance to move the story along, one sentence at a time.

At George's suggestion, we tried it in the workshop and it was a lot of fun, especially since nobody tried to be funny. We did, however, encounter a few run-on sentences. I could imagine this game turning into a marathon event.

Perhaps more subtle are the creative responses called forth when devising winning strategies for more organized games. Games made up on the spot, such as during trips in the family car, represent yet another challenge to creative juices. Finally, there are the "performances," impromptu and otherwise, that children are welcome to stage for the rest of the family that draw on their talent for satire and mimicry.

The Value of Improvisation
Since the fearless family endorses risk taking and creativity in family play, spontaneity is enhanced and imagination is encouraged. This is the stuff of improvisation.

In fact the fun-filled family interaction will often resemble that of a successful improvisational troupe. There is the palpable chemistry of mutual support and respect. There is the tendency to trust one another without question. There is the willingness to embrace uncritically the "premise" suggested by one's partner (or playmate), so long as it is within the bounds of acceptable behavior. And of course there are the inevitable frequent outbursts of laughter.

We need not belabor the point that the ability to improvise (to "think on one's feet") is of great value in all aspects of life, inside and outside the family.

The Value of Celebration

In the fearless family, play is always a form of celebration. On the surface of its fun-filled rituals the prevalence of laughter and joyful interaction speaks for itself. But there are deeper currents of celebration as well.

The verbal and non-verbal expression of love and respect, that is so much a part of the fun we are advocating, is a quiet celebration of gratitude for each member. Thus, fun-based family life promotes an enduring sense of gratitude for the safety, comfort and security it provides.

In life, the value of celebration is that it reminds us of those things and persons for which we are most grateful. Gratitude is always a prelude to greater joy. This is an everyday experience in the fearless, fun-filled family.

It was just a weekend family meal at our son's house, when, during the saying of grace, three-year-old grandson, William, voiced the following addendum: "And God bless Nanny for bringing the dessert!"

The Value of Flexibility

The fun-based family teaches flexibility, a valuable attribute of successful people. Holding fast to one's principles, while remaining flexible, may seem at times to require the skills of a contortionist. It's just an every day experience in the fearless family.

Many people view flexibility as a sign of weakness. A moment's reflection tells us that it is usually the rigid tree that snaps during a windstorm. People, like trees, are more likely to break when they are brittle and inflexible.

Flexibility is a chief characteristic of a fun-filled family. It is the dysfunctional family that is rigid and devoid of fun. Consequently functional family members learn that flexibility does not undermine progress. It enhances it. In encouraging and allowing the spontaneity of emotion and activity that we previously described as reminiscent of improvisation, the fun-filled family demonstrates how focus and flexibility work seamlessly together.

The Value of Teamwork

The experience of teamwork is essential to the realization of one's true relationship to the grand scheme of things in this world. Nowhere is there a greater opportunity to learn this than in the fearless, fun-filled family.

Teamwork begins with the non-exclusionary character of family play, which assures that everyone has a significant role in the game or ritual. Each person, young or old, is appreciated for what he or she can do to contribute to the fun.

Team spirit grows stronger as family members "root" for one another, applauding and supporting every good effort. And, of course, nearly every "game" the family plays illustrates the benefits of collaboration to achieve maximal success.

A colleague specializing in oncology shared a reminiscence at a recent Fun Factor workshop. He recalled family games of Monopoly that would go on sometimes for days.

He especially remembered his Uncle Bob, who was notorious for making creative deals and alliances "on the side." There would be moments in the game when Uncle Bob was in cahoots with so many people, on so many levels, that even he could not tell if he was winning or losing. But Uncle Bob always had fun making the game more "interesting."

The Value of Competition

It is said that competition is a necessary evil in life. I agree it is necessary, but I think that, like stress, its "evilness" depends on how much of it we face and what we do with it.

Some purists, surmising that competition poisons the well in fearless family play, will advocate that families should confine themselves to non-competitive games. I disagree, although I have nothing against non-competitive games.

To me the issue isn't the presence or absence of competition.

It is the spirit in which it is engaged. In the functional, fun-filled family, competition is part of the fun. As such, it makes the process more interesting and engaging. As we've seen, the process is always more important than the outcome. In addition, competition is a stimulus to excellent performance. Doing one's best adds to the fun of any experience.

Focusing too heavily on the outcome is where families can get into trouble with competition. When the final score becomes more important than the fun of playing, that's problematical. It encourages playing not to lose, which always places limitations on fun. But the solution is not the elimination of competition. For one thing, that's probably impossible. For another, that's like throwing the baby out with the bath water. There is nothing inherently wrong with competition.

The solution is to regard competition in the spirit of fun. Fun-filled family members are encouraged to celebrate effort, regardless of the score, because the fun is in interacting with one another. Preoccupation with winning is usually a sign that there is a scarcity of recognition and appreciation of effort overall. That is a communication problem, which should be easy to diagnose and fix in a fun-based family.

Chapter Five

MAKING WORK NOT WORK AT WORK

We have said that the family is the launching pad for life, the test tube in which we learn to like or dislike ourselves. We've seen the desirable values that are celebrated in the fun-filled family and reviewed many of the behaviors that are taught and reinforced. Up until now we have focused upon the development of self-esteem and self-discipline in the early years of family life. Now we turn our attention to the issue of self-fulfillment. For this we must broaden our perspective.

Having described in detail the characteristics and benefits of the Fun Factor in family life, we are ready to consider how effectively these strategies and values extrapolate into the world beyond. It is natural and desirable for children, as they grow older, to seek relationships and meaning outside the comforting confines of the immediate family. The nest is a launching pad, not a destination.

As important as family is, at some point it becomes too restrictive for the maturing young adult it has been nurturing. He seeks freedom to grow beyond his comfortable family role, in order to further discover and define himself. He needs new relationships and new opportunities. The world at large is beckoning, challenging him to tackle its many mysteries.

What role will this emerging young adult choose to play on the larger stage? Having counted for something in fun-filled family life, he must now take his skills to a more spacious arena and attempt to make a difference there. It's as though everything that transpired within the family was a prelude to life in the world beyond.

His emergence is not a sudden event. It is a gradual assumption of independence, sometimes halting, at other times rapid, a natural concomitant to his growth and maturation over the years. However, there are certain moments in time that bring the transforming process into bold prominence, forcing the family to recognize and grapple with the changes that are occurring. The beginning of school, an overnight stay at a friend's home, a first date, getting a job and going off to college are examples of such signal moments. Some can be painful and frightening, threatening the coherence and integrity of the family unit.

As with the portentous first smile between infant and parent, these moments hold great potential for fear or fun. And like the initial smile the issue is equally critical for parent and child. For the family that has lived fearlessly by the Fun Factor, this is not the time to abandon humor. Cultivated over many years, the "habit" of laughing together can pay huge dividends now.

That is because family fun has no equal as an antidote to fear in these moments. The family which gives up its reliance on fun by yielding to misgivings about things "left undone" or running from fears of the unknown, uncontrollable "outside world," risks eroding the very foundation of its unity and security, just when it is most needed. It is the simple spirit of the "first smile" that can sustain a family while it successfully meets these "new" challenges.

Mark, the oldest of three children, recalled how his family had dealt with his first date. His memories of the teasing he received from his siblings stood out strongly.

"My girlfriend's name was Nancy," he reported. "I can still hear my little brother saying, 'He's looking *fancy* for *Nancy!*' as I emerged from my bedroom wearing my best shirt and reeking from about three gallons of the cologne my dad had lent to me."

He hastened to add that his sister participated in the teasing as well, by "threatening" to tag along as a chaperone.

"What I remember most of all," he concluded, "was how the teasing made me forget about my nervousness. And, when my father hugged me and slipped some extra cash into my pocket, it felt like I wasn't taking this scary step entirely on my own. It made me feel at home, even though I was going out, if that makes any sense."

Sandra, the youngest in a family of five children, was telling her cancer support group about the time when her oldest sister went off to college.

"It was very sad at first. It felt like she had died. Her room was so empty. I missed her so much. I would sometimes just sit in her bedroom and cry.

The first time she came back home was at Thanksgiving. By then I was, if anything, angry. I had gotten used to her being gone and I resented her coming back. I was going to show her that we were having even more fun in the family without her.

I know now that I was really just afraid that I had lost her; that she'd forgotten about me.

My fears quickly disappeared when we began teasing and laughing right where we had left off three months back. She wasn't home more than five minutes before our playfulness took over. I found it irresistible and my plans to punish her with a cold shoulder, melted immediately.

She hadn't changed, nor had I. We hadn't lost anything. The time apart had not undermined our family ties.

That's the way it still is to this day, no matter how much time elapses between visits."

It cannot be overemphasized that the emancipation process to which we refer is a two-way street. The challenge is not solely to the emerging offspring. Perhaps more than at any other time since the first smile, parents are prey to strong fears. How they choose between fear and fun will wield great influence during this transition time. Reluctance to let go may communicate fear and uncertainty, undermining their child's confidence. A spirit of fun encourages all to celebrate the miracle of the growth that is taking place.

It is also important to recognize that there is a strong element of grief shared by parents and children around the nest-leaving rituals. Both sides are called upon to let go. Levels of intimacy are threatened and exclusiveness of relationship must be given up.

If the family has been promoting and enjoying the Fun Factor all along, it will naturally find humor of great assistance here. If it has not chosen to be fun-based, it will be extremely difficult, if not impossible, to resort to humor successfully at this late date. The opportunity to call forth this resource may be long gone.

Later in the book we will discuss the relationship of humor with grief in more detail. For now, let it suffice to repeat once more that humor is a most effective resource for helping families get through these often painful transitions.

Choosing Work

The occasion of leaving the nest is a true self-defining experience. Decisions made during this metamorphosis are likely to set a course for many years, if not for life. Careers and relationships hang in the balance. Ultimately, options will be open or closed, according to the limitations imposed by the initial choices.

Nevertheless, the attitude and spirit with which these early adult decisions are made are actually more important than their content or direction. For example, the spirit of fear creates a desperate pressure to get everything right the first time. Miscalculations are unacceptable. On the other hand, the spirit of fun allows for flexibility, which creates a certain tolerance for mistakes.

A family that simultaneously teaches flexibility and focus is best at preparing its offspring for this phase of life. Leaving the nest with fun does not trivialize the moment. To the contrary, just like everything else in the fun-filled family, it enriches the experience and makes it more meaningful.

One of the most important challenges in life is choosing an

occupation. For most adults, work is essential to self-fulfillment. How will a young person choose his work? Will the family support any choice or will it impose its expectations? The fearless family is more likely to offer the opportunity for the person to define the job, rather than the job defining the person.

When a child has been raised in a fun-based family atmosphere, how will the benefits translate into the broader arena? Will the values and skills she learned be an asset or a liability in the cold, cruel world? Let's describe a prototypical young adult who has enjoyed, from birth, the daily benefits of the Fun Factor. How might she present herself, poised to venture forth from her family into the fray?

What would this young lady be like if we met her for the first time at a social occasion? I suggest that she would be a friendly, outgoing person, with a ready smile and a propensity for laughter. She would be an effective communicator, as well as a careful listener. I believe we would describe her as self-confident, but not overly caught up in ideas of self-importance. While keeping an open mind, she would be gracious and respectful toward other points of view. We would see clear evidence of optimism, enthusiasm and hope in her demeanor. She would likely demonstrate a creative mind and be able to think well "on her feet."

Taking it a step further, what might we learn about this young person if we continued our relationship with her over time? With repeated contacts, I think we would discover that, despite her open-mindedness and flexibility, she was well grounded, disciplined and focused, with a clear vision of her personal priorities. We would soon find that whenever she gave her word, we could count on it. Trusting the accuracy of her intuition, she would be willing to take risks and would welcome unexpected occurrences as enjoyable surprises. She would demonstrate the capacity for readily accepting responsibility for her mistakes.

As we spent even more time with her, we would notice that she kept things simple by not holding grudges and always looked for the positive elements of any situation. Consequently, we would be impressed with her personal resilience and her ability to maintain a balanced perspective. Another characteristic we might observe is her love of competition and her tendency to thrive on it. Yet, at the same time, we would find her to be a valuable team player, able to celebrate and enjoy the accomplishments of others around her.

I admit that we have created an idealized character. No one person could possibly cover all those bases. The point is that every trait described can be traced directly back to one or more of the learning opportunities that are abundantly available in fearless, fun-filled family life.

Judging from this, which energy would we expect her to draw upon for making important decisions – fun or fear? It would be understandable if she chose fear. After all, she is beset with many competing pressures and expectations, not to mention countless uncertainties.

Will she minimize risk by choosing the safest path? Fun-filled family life has taught her to be unafraid of risk. Will she make decisions designed to avoid the disapproval of other people? Her experience with the Fun Factor has given her confidence in the still small voice of her own intuition. Is she likely to grab at the first opportunity, for fear of ending up with nothing? Her fearless family life has provided her with faith in the long-term perspective.

It is more likely that the young person we have described will choose fun as her guide in making critical decisions. She will gravitate toward opportunities and situations that fit her own interests and talents. She will be confident of her skills and clear about her priorities. It is unlikely she will ever become overly dependent upon her occupation to define who she is. She is more apt to allow her personal characteristics to influence and shape her work.

Thus, her decisions will often boil down quite simply to one prevailing criterion—"Would it be fun for me?" Only a person raised in an environment in which fun was strongly endorsed and respected could ever consider that to be a responsible question. Yet the wisdom of the question would be so natural to her that she might not even consciously realize its influence.

This brings us back to the distinction between simple and easy. Her decisions will not be easy, but if she remembers what she's learned, they will be simpler than she might otherwise imagine. In fact, keeping things "as simple as possible, but no simpler" is a key strategy for anyone who chooses to take fun with her into the workplace.

Why would anyone want to consider taking the Fun Factor onto his job? What makes us think that, just because fun proves to be valuable at home, it would have any benefits for the workplace? The answer to that question is itself quite simple. Work is, for better or worse, an extension of family structure, with one exception. At work, the "kids" aren't as helpless as in the family. Other than that, the two situations are pretty much the same. Whatever you experienced in family life will probably hold true for the work environment as well.

That's because the truth doesn't change. If fear limited your options and skills in family life, it will do the same at work. Fun, on the other hand, will enhance any effort in both arenas. If it works in microcosm, it will surely work in macrocosm. If anything, the "spotlight" of the larger stage only serves to illuminate it more.

In family the interactions that we've described have been somewhat subjective. A fearless healthy family rarely sees fit to require its members to punch a time clock. And you won't see many meetings dedicated to wider profit margins or increased market share. However, such scrutiny of effort and productivity is commonplace in the workplace. And the more carefully one measures, the better fun looks as a resource.

All objective measures in the workplace confirm what we learned in our examination of fun-filled family life. When we have fun at work, absenteeism and turnover of personnel are reduced, while morale and productivity are enhanced. The bottom line is that fun makes us better and healthier at work, just as it did in our families. The only reason not to bring fun to work is if you don't want to be successful.

Remember, we already have documented proof that having fun reduces stress, boosts immunity, relieves pain, decreases anxiety, prevents depression, rests the brain, enhances communication, inspires creativity, maintains hope and bolsters morale. Think of any job, even the worst you can imagine, and tell me why you wouldn't want all those benefits while you were doing it.

Fun boils down to one word—energy. Substitute the word energy for fun, then ask yourself, "Do I want more or less energy when I'm working?" With the possible exception of Robin Williams, we all could use more, not less.

The failure to understand that fun is nothing more than pure energy has caused many to balk at the idea of having more fun at work. Craig, a 47-year-old business owner, had this to say when asked about humor in his workplace:

"I've read all that stuff about laughter being good for business, but I don't buy it. Maybe it helps if you're selling ice cream or toys, but my experience is different.

"I run my business on a tight margin. The competition is fierce. We don't have the luxury of making mistakes. I tell my people, 'If you want to play games, do it on your own time.' The only way to survive these days is to run a tight ship.

"Of course I'd like to have more fun. Who wouldn't? I don't enjoy always worrying about the bottom line. But if I let them play on the assembly line, we'd lose our focus and our competitive edge, not to mention, before you know it, somebody gets hurt.

"If we lose our competitive edge, then we have no jobs to offer. Which would you rather have, a good job or a good time?"

Craig's words are important for at least two reasons. First, he's raising an issue that deserves an answer, namely how do we reconcile playfulness with serious responsibilities? Second, he represents approximately two-thirds of all the CEOs and managers in American business today, men and women who acknowledge the generalizations about humor's benefit in the workplace, but find it too risky to encourage its incorporation into their particular operations. We will devote the next chapter to helping these individuals. However, in the meantime, we must recognize that they represent a significant challenge to the rest of us.

If the statistics are correct, the chances are better than 50/50 that you are going to be working for someone who thinks as Craig does. This means, if you plan to enjoy the benefits of more fun in your work, you are on your own. You won't be getting a lot of help or encouragement from upper management. You'll have to do it for yourself. That's not as bad as it might seem, because, as you will learn by reading further, even in those instances when the boss is supportive, you're still pretty much on your own. Having fun is an "inside job," requiring a lot of self-discipline.

Now, just before we get to the "hands-on" practicalities of making work more fun, I recommend we pause to allow you to ask yourself a few basic questions that will be of immeasurable help. What prompted you to choose the line of work you are doing or planning to do? What factors are compelling you? Are you being pulled or pushed?

Where did you first get the idea that you wanted to do the work you have chosen? Who or what influenced you? Why do you think this work would be good for you? What will you accomplish that meets your need for self-fulfillment?

What are your specific goals? Why? What is your timetable? Is it realistic? How are you defining success? How will you measure your progress? Where does your work fit in with the rest of your life? How does it enrich the other parts of your life?

These are important questions because they will help you define the parameters of your work. They will force you to think clearly and honestly about your goals and priorities. Your answers will give you the perspective by which to keep track of your progress and keep your life in balance. You see, *fun will make you successful, but it still falls to you to define your success.*

Remember that, although the relationship between success and fun has been well established, it's easy to get the sequence backwards. Having fun first is what leads to success, not the other way around. If we bypass fun to concentrate exclusively on success, we will find that success without fun promotes fear.

By the way, these questions are as critical for those "graduating" from a fun-filled family, as for anyone else. Coming from a fun-based background may make certain challenges easier to face, but it doesn't excuse one from the footwork necessary to be successful. Asking tough basic questions about your motivation for your work is definitely an example of necessary footwork.

Don't assume you know what's pushing you toward that job. Make sure it's not fear. Insist on fun-based motives.

Peter came to me for help during his third year of medical school. Unable to sleep at night, he was having problems with constant fatigue.

Although he was doing well in school, his problem had begun to affect his performance by causing him to fall asleep in class and during clinical procedures. He was afraid that his frequent "catnaps" were getting worse and, in time, would get him in trouble.

As he talked about his medical training, it was clear that he had drawn great satisfaction from "getting through" the first two years, which were filled with hours of pressure-packed reading and studying. His current problem didn't arise until he began his third year clinical assignments, in which he was expected to learn at the bedside rather than from the book.

He admitted that he wasn't enjoying patient contact as much as he thought he would. He felt overwhelmed by the intimacy and the responsibility. This led me to ask about how he decided on medicine as a career.

"I owe it to my family and to myself to become a doctor," was his reply. "My brother was killed by a drunken driver when I was a sophomore in high school, He was in his third year of college, home for the holidays, and was coming to pick me up at the movies the night the accident happened. I know it's crazy, but I have always felt he'd still be alive today, if I hadn't asked him to pick me up that night.

"The accident devastated all of us. He had been planning to be a doctor for as long as I can remember. So, I decided that I would go to medical school in his place. I want to become the doctor the world has been deprived of by his death. Nobody put any pressure on me. It was my own idea."

I asked him what he would be doing if he weren't trying to fill that void. It took some urging to get an answer. Reluctantly he shared with me that he wanted to be a painter. He had always wanted to be an artist of some kind.

Over months of intensive, sometimes agonizing, dialogue, Peter came to realize that he really wasn't comfortable in medicine and that the best way to honor his brother and his parents would be to pursue his unique gifts as an artist.

Today, he has a successful career in graphic design and is highly respected as a teacher and mentor of young artists.

Now let us turn to practicalities. What strategies can we actually implement to successfully turn work into "not work"?

Smile More Often

This is perhaps the most basic strategy for fun in the workplace. It is in fact absolutely foolproof. If you make it a priority to smile more frequently while you're at work, you will be amazed at the results.

"When I'm at work I only talk to people who are already smiling," volunteered Betsy, a secretary working in a university research center. "When you ask somebody who's not smiling how they are doing, you usually get a complaint or something negative. Either that or they're too preoccupied. I feel like I'm interrupting something of dire importance. It brings me down. I don't need that. I take a smile as a signal that something positive can be transacted."

She continued, "Then one day it dawned on me that perhaps others felt the same way when approaching me. So, I tried to smile more. Guess what? Since I started that, I find more people smiling at me. Life is like a big mirror. The number of smiling people I see, is a reflection of how much I'm smiling."

Frequent smiling is a strategy that is best begun early each day , prior to setting foot in your workplace. In fact, a good time to initiate this technique is first thing in the morning. In his inimitable style, W.C. Fields gave good advice when he said, "Smile first thing every morning, and get it over with!"

I recommend that you begin your morning routine by stretching all your smile muscles. For this, you will want to refer to the protocol that we described in Chapter One. If you can start your day smiling you will enjoy the other rituals that follow. That first smile will give you more energy than the healthy breakfast you never have enough time for. The morning news, if you must have it, will not burden you with its negativity, if you read it with a smile. You'll find that you'll have more resilience and tolerance for the actual trip to work. Those other drivers may still be idiots, but you won't take it so personally.

All of which is to say, that, if you start smiling early enough, by the time you get to work, you will already be having a successful day. It is much easier to perpetuate success, than to "kick start" it from a standstill when you get to your workstation.

At this point, it's a matter of remembering to ride the horse that got you this far—your simple, yet powerful, smile. Don't send it out to pasture. Stay on it. Keep your focus on smiling no matter what you're called upon to do. And remember, even if you don't feel like smiling, faking it does a great deal of good.

Let me give you some thoughts that might help you maintain your smile focus. I know that one thing that drags our spirits down at work is that we feel insignificant. We don't feel like we can make a difference. Well, consider what Gene had to say about smiling at a recent cancer support group:

"I think that if everybody on earth would smile at the same time, we could heal the world. But it ain't gonna happen according to any plan. Just synchronizing our watches would be a major problem.

So, if it ever happens it's going to have to be by coincidence, or a miracle, if you want to call it that. Now, what if we came real close to pulling it off just by coincidence, and you were the only one who wasn't smiling? Wouldn't you feel terrible to be holding us all back like that?"

The next time you feel insignificant, think of Gene's hypothesis, and at least smile.

Here's another thought to reinforce your commitment to smile as often as you can think of it. If I was walking past your desk or your workspace and you didn't have a smile, I would assume, like Betsy, that you were preoccupied with something on your mind;

much too "busy" to hear anything as trivial as my latest story about my grandchildren. But, if you're smiling, I might take the time to tell you that about my grandson Jordan's visit to his pediatrician. While she was looking in his ears, he said, "Doctor, can I tell you something?

"Of course, Jordan," she answered. "What do you want to tell me?"

"If you pick up a squirrel or a chipmunk," he warned her, "They'll bite you."

Now that is not a joke. It's just a pleasant story about a six-year old boy being six years old. If I shared it with you, we would both get a few seconds of fun out of it.

Here's the point. I promise you that the interchange would only happen if you were smiling. If not, we both would miss it. It's just not worth the intrusion into your serious demeanor. So, how many of those brief moments of fun do you miss every day because you're not smiling? Ten? Twenty? Who can tell! Maybe if you plugged that leak, it would be enough to make a difference in your level of fun.

Folks, smiling more often is not rocket science. It's just simple commitment and discipline. Instead of agreeing to smile whenever something is amusing, commit to smiling every time you become aware that you are not. Take back control of your smile and you'll have more fun at work.

Always Look for the Pony

Here's another simple strategy that can't fail to provide you with more fun at work, regardless of the circumstances. This one is purely a matter of sustaining energy and discipline. Looking for the pony is not a philosophical mind game. Like the little boy in the joke, we can be assured that there is a pony in every pile of manure.

It makes no difference whether the proverbial glass is half full or half empty. There is a 100 percent guarantee of a pony in every pile. Maintaining your optimism doesn't require one stitch of faith. It only requires a tireless resolve to find the pony.

When we were both seniors in college, my friend Tom

suffered a devastating loss. His twin sister was killed in a traffic accident. All of us who were close to him were terribly shaken by his tragedy.

At the funeral, I noticed Tom seemed to need less comforting than the rest of us. When I asked him how he was holding up so well, he didn't hesitate with his answer.

"Cliff, I know there's a gift in all this for me. I just haven't found it yet."

"Your faith must be very strong," I commented.

"It isn't faith," he corrected me. "The gift is here for sure. I just have to find it."

Years later he wrote me a letter to tell me he had "found" it. He admitted that, prior to his sister's death, he had been something of a Lone Ranger, not allowing anyone to get too close. Over the years, he realized that losing his sister had taught him the value of spending ample time with those people you love and who love you in return.

He is happily married (something he had predicted would never happen, since he came from a broken home), with two children and is enjoying success as a general surgeon.

Back at the time of his sister's death, Tom's words had confused and unnerved me. As I learned more about human psychology, I came to think of them as examples of an extreme denial of painful grief. I was wrong. He was wise enough to know that, despite the pain he was experiencing, it would only be a matter of time until he received something of value from it. He was right.

This strategy is not "mind over matter." It's a pragmatic discipline based on the truth. Sometimes the ponies are very hard to find. It can take years. At other times, you will see them almost as soon as you are willing to look. In either case you are more likely to find the pony if you are looking for it.

And even before you find it, expecting it to be there can change your energy from reluctance and pessimism to enthusiasm and optimism. You tell me which is more fun.

Finally, I want to point out that this strategy will do nothing to change the character of the situation. Tom's loss was very real and very painful to him, despite his insightfulness. Manure is still manure, whether or not you're looking for a pony. What we are talking about here is making the inevitable more tolerable. Enthusiasm is a relative thing, more or less.

So, the next time you face a pile of manure in your path or on your desk at work (Sounds familiar, doesn't it?), be assured that it is hiding a gift for you and, before doing anything else, remember to ask, "Where's the pony in this pile?"

Let Go Frequently

At first blush, this strategy might sound like a bad idea. After all, American ideology promises that you can achieve anything if you are willing to work hard enough and long enough for it. The catch is in the phrase, "work hard enough." Work too little and you are bound to lose out; but work too hard and failure is just as certain. Most of us don't let go often enough to explore the middle ground.

David, a friend and a psychiatrist, was our houseguest for the weekend. After breakfast on Saturday morning, I announced that I was going to give one of our horses a training session.

"Can I come along and watch?" asked David.

"Of course," I responded, glad for the company.

The horse was a yearling named Darby. I caught him easily in his pasture. Maybe I was in a hurry or just showing off, but for some reason I did not take Darby to the training ring. Instead, I hooked him up to the lunge line and started to work with him right there in his pasture.

Darby was on his best behavior. He was paying attention and responding to all my commands, as if I were a master trainer. Soon David, who had been sitting on the fence watching all this, asked, "Could I try working with him?"

"Have you ever done this before?" I countered.

"Oh yeah," he assured me, "I was raised around horses."

"Be my guest," I said, offering him the lunge line and the whip.

David chose to initiate things by cracking the whip in the air. This startled Darby, who pricked his ears, arched his neck, and took off across the pasture, with David in tow.

"Let go!" I yelled. But David held on tight. And Darby just went faster.

"Let go!" I yelled even louder. This time, after being dragged the length of a football field, David let go.

I ran to him and found him essentially unhurt, but very embarrassed. As he brushed himself off, I asked him, "Why didn't you let go sooner, David?"

"I thought I could stop him," he answered. As he spoke those words I think they sounded as absurd to him as they did to me. It's pretty hard to stop an 800-pound animal at full gallop with anything less than a cannon.

"I thought I could stop him!" Have you ever thought or said anything that absurd when faced with an overwhelming situation? I know I have often found myself standing up to an onrushing problem, knowing in my mind I had no chance, but unwilling to admit it—unwilling to let go.

Let me tell you what I learned that day with David. As soon as I made sure David wasn't injured, I turned to Darby. What would you guess he was doing? He was calmly grazing. You see, as soon as David let go, Darby stopped running. Apparently there was something about dragging a psychiatrist behind him that was spooking the horse all along. I just picked up his line and led him quietly back to the barn, as if nothing unusual had happened.

I think that's a metaphor for life. When we finally have the good sense to let go, problems quite often take care of themselves. Even if they don't, the respite might give us a different perspective, a new angle. Even if the problem persists and we have to get back in the ring with it, we will be fresher for having given ourselves the opportunity to catch our breath.

Something else occurs to me as I think about that Saturday morning. It was only when David let go that I was able to catch up to him and render assistance, if needed. Before that, all I could do was helplessly watch the debacle.

Here's a second metaphor for life. How many times do we miss out on the help and support our family and friends can offer, because we won't let go and they can't "catch up" to render assistance? Letting go is simple, but not easy.

∼

A hiker lost his balance and fell over the edge of a steep and high cliff. At the last minute he saved himself by grabbing a small branch growing out of the sheer rock wall.

Dangling helplessly over a 2000-foot ravine, he began yelling. "Help! Help! Is there anyone up there?"

Suddenly he heard a booming voice. "I'll help you."

"Who are you?" asked the man.

"I'm God," answered the voice.

"Oh, thank you, thank you," said the grateful man. "I knew my faith would someday be rewarded. What should I do?"

"Just let go and I'll catch you," instructed the voice.

"What?" exclaimed the man.

"I said just let go and I'll catch you," God repeated.

The man paused, then yelled, "Is there anyone else up there?"

∼

As we learned from observing fun-filled family interaction, letting go is more than an effective strategy for problem solving. It is also an effective resource for strengthening our human relationships. Carrying resentments and grudges into the workplace will bog you down and stifle your productivity. Does that sound like fun?

Free yourself. Have more fun. Practice letting go frequently.

Keep It Fresh

A wise man once wrote, "The only difference between a rut and a grave is the depth." There is a certain amount of repetition in any job. Quality control and "brand" expectation demand it. Nobody wants to open a can of Coke and taste something different than the one they had yesterday. Nevertheless, it is a good idea to frequently alter whatever we can about our work to avoid sinking into a mindless rut of routine.

While Jerry Lewis was touring in the musical "Damn Yankees," I frequently joined him to present our "Laughter and Healing" seminar at hospitals and medical schools in the various cities he played. Since our seminars were in the daytime, I usually flew in the night before in time to accompany him to the theatre. Consequently, I saw "Damn Yankees" dozens of times.

I never tired of seeing it. That's because, inspired by Mr. Lewis himself, the cast never tired of performing it. To keep the energy fresh, Jerry would play tricks on his fellow performers. He would "punctuate" a serious line with one of his trademark funny faces, which could be seen only by the other actors, not the audience. Or he would read the same line in a different voice each night. There was no end to his subtle variations, all of which were funny only to those familiar with the expected routine.

Members of the cast, taking their cue from Jerry, would delight in playing tricks back on him. At one point in the first act, Jerry had to look off to stage left and describe something unseen to the audience. Every night someone or something would be in the stage left wings to distract him and throw him off-stride. I can't describe all of the visual "treats" they arranged for him because this is a "G" rated book. Suffice it to say that he rarely got through that moment in the show without breaking up. Many a night the show going on backstage was funnier than the one seen by the audience.

To put and keep fun in your work you must break up the routine wherever and whenever possible. Like the smiling strategy, this may be something that begins even before arriving at your workplace. How many different routes have you taken to get to your job? There's room for variation there. Do you always use the same form of transportation? You could occasionally do something different.

If your work does not require a specific uniform, you may want to be creative in your attire, remembering that the strategy is for your own good. It is not necessary to "publicize" all of your grooming modifications. If it's fun for you to wear a diaper occasionally, nobody else has to know about it. I think I speak for everyone involved when I say we'd rather not know about it.

Then, once you are on the job, try to do something new every day. Alter your schedule so that you don't do things in the same sequence every time. Rearrange your desk drawers so that you have to think where things are located. Redecorate your workspace often. Maintain your peripheral vision by keeping an eye on the outside world, not just on your desk.

Train yourself to abhor sameness. Don't get too attached to any one way. This goes for your thought processes as well. Challenge all your assumptions. Don't take for granted that "business as usual" is the best way, just because it's familiar and comfortable. Keep in mind that most of your thoughts are merely assumptions based on your best guess or on what somebody told you (probably an assumption once removed).

This strategy will stimulate new thinking and increase your fun. You will become more creative and innovative. Since challenging prevailing assumptions is the chief mechanism of all humor, you will be exercising your humor nature as well.

Perhaps most important of all, keeping it fresh will prepare you for the inevitable changes coming your way. Make no mistake about it. Change is inevitable, except from a vending machine. Physical and mental routines can lull you into a false sense of security tempting you to resist change—a fear-based strategy that is destined to fail.

Make It a Game

An excellent way to put fun into any activity is to make a game of it. This has been illustrated time and again in our descriptions of fearless fun-filled family life. There is no task so onerous that it could not be made more interesting if turned into a game.

Frank, a salesman, is on the road most of the time. He says, "The bane of my existence is calling in for my voice mail every day. It helps if I make a game out of it. I keep a log of the time it takes from the first dialed number to the hang-up at the end.

"I try to beat my record for brevity, which now stands at 25 seconds. If there are a lot of messages, I have a backup plan. I go for the longest time. My current marathon record is 14 minutes and 37 seconds. Whenever I can beat either of these marks, I treat myself to a movie or a ball game.

"It doesn't exactly make it fun to call in, but either way, I have something to shoot for."

Virtually anything can be made into a game by finding a way to keep score formally or informally. When a New York critic wrote that Jerry Lewis "hit a home run every night" in the show "Damn Yankees," we kept a count of each performance, and when he reached 756 home runs, the cast gave him a trophy during the curtain call, for breaking Hank Aaron's record. It was just another way to make some fun out of the drudgery of life on the road.

Remember what we learned from the back seat of the fun-filled family car? We need not put off fun until we get there. We can have it en route. Usually this involves making a game of it. And, often this requires nothing more than a mental adjustment. Taking the time to do this will make tedious tasks go faster.

You don't always have to keep this strategy to yourself. If more than one can play your game, invite your fellow workers to join in. You'll be surprised how often they will be eager to do so, while adding some innovative wrinkles for you in the bargain. Playing phone tag is a frequent opportunity for game playing. For another example, you might invite a co-worker to join you in a game of avoiding certain "buzzwords", a reverse version of Groucho's "say the magic word" on *You Bet Your Life*. Offer a prize for whoever can go the longest without mentioning the words "win/win situation" or "twenty-four/seven."

The bottom line is making it fun and keeping it simple. When you do, it can be a win/win situation for everybody. Oops! I owe you a prize.

Chapter Six

Creating a Fun Factor Organization

In the last chapter, we focused upon the individual worker who intends to have more fun at his or her job. Now we turn our attention to corporate strategies for creating a fun environment in the workplace. In this chapter we will discuss the leadership techniques that support fun.

Business leaders generally agree in principle that humor is a good thing to encourage. In a recent survey 96 percent of responding executives said they believed that people with a sense of humor do better at their jobs than those who have little or no sense of humor. However, when they think of using humor in the workplace, most bosses are stymied by their failure to understand its practical applications.

When we quoted Craig in Chapter Five, we observed that he raised some legitimate questions reflecting the thoughts and concerns shared by more than half of the business leaders in America today. Most of these concerns stem from a misperception that humor encourages irresponsible behavior. In this respect, leaders of companies share the same concerns as many parents in the home. They ask, "If I support and encourage humor in my workplace, won't that send the wrong message?" They fear that people will lose respect for their authority and for them personally, and will become distracted from the serious responsibilities the company must meet. "If I lose control of the situation, the ship will be rudderless."

It would have helped if more of these CEOs and managers had been raised in fearless fun-filled families. They would have learned first-hand how responsible and reliable humor really can be. Many of their fears and concerns would already be set to rest. My hunch is that's what happened with the relatively few business leaders who stand out as examples of success in implementing humor-based business strategies. Alas, Herb Kelleher, the CEO of Southwest Airlines, represents the exception, not the rule.

Why should I use humor in my business?

The reason to utilize the Fun Factor is as simple for the organization as it is for the individual. By making the effort to install and maintain the Fun Factor in your work environment, you will make your company more successful.

What do we mean by successful? That's for you to define. Whether you choose profitability, growth, increased market share, expanding markets, increasing relevance to the community, or any combination of these and other factors as your measuring stick, it doesn't matter. Regardless of the measures used, the success of any business comes down to one indispensable factor—satisfied customers. You can't succeed without satisfied and enthusiastic customers.

The Fun Factor will produce satisfied customers in droves. Why? Because putting fun into the workplace insures enthusiastic, satisfied employees. And happy employees are the best guarantee of happy customers. It's just that simple, but, as we've said many times, not so easy. If it were easy everybody would be doing it.

The Fun Factor creates employee satisfaction because it puts the employee first, above product, above marketing, above profit, and, yes, even above the customer. The truth is that *putting employee satisfaction first makes customer satisfaction last.. and last.. and last.* No wonder the McDonald's company likes the slogan, "We love to see you smile." They know it pertains to employees as well as customers.

Rose, a 28-year-old hairdresser, spoke up in a recent workshop about her boss. "After I'd been working at the salon for about a year, I encountered my first problem customer. She was an older woman with a condescending disposition, who was impossible to satisfy. In the first place, she had a habit of arriving late for her appointments, so that I would have to work fast to avoid being late for my other appointments. On top of that, she would gripe constantly about how much she resented young people, never stopping to consider that I might take some of her negative comments personally. It was certainly hard not to. But above everything else, she never was happy with my work. Yet she kept coming back to me.

"It got to the point that I was dreading going to work on the days I had this woman on my schedule. I asked my boss, who owns the salon, what suggestions he might have to help me handle the situation. I expected he would counsel me on how to deflect her negativity and perhaps encourage me to develop a 'thicker skin' toward her personal criticism.

"Instead he surprised me. He suggested that I simply tell her that my work schedule was changing and that I would not be able to continue to do her hair. He recommended that I give her the names of one or two other salons where there might be some openings.

"I was grateful for the advice, but I had to ask him why, as the owner of our salon, he was counseling me to, in effect, turn away business. I'll never forget his answer.

"He simply said, 'You are more important than any one customer. Customers come and go, but you're here every day. You're a part of our family. If you're unhappy, we're unhappy. We can easily get another customer, but we can't get another you.'

"I don't remember ever feeling that valuable to anyone. When I own my own salon, I hope I can make my employees feel that appreciated."

That is an atmosphere of fun in action. Not in terms of laughter or jokes. But do you doubt for a minute the enthusiasm Rose now has for working in that salon, for that boss?

The great Hollywood director, Joseph Mankiewicz, was once asked to name the key factor in a successful movie shoot. He answered, "Create an atmosphere for fun on the set, and you'll get great work." When the workplace atmosphere is fun, employees want to come to work. Company morale improves and absenteeism decreases. Performance is enhanced and productivity goes up. As employees gain greater satisfaction from their work, turnover rates go down. We know it is more cost effective to retain an experienced employee than to train a new one.

A quick review of humor's documented role in reducing stress, boosting immunity, relieving pain, decreasing anxiety, preventing depression, putting the brain at rest, enhancing communication, inspiring creativity, maintaining hope and bolstering morale, explains why it produces such desirable results. All of those effects, in one way or another, contribute to a thriving and successful workforce.

Creating the Atmosphere
There are three things to remember if you want to create and maintain an atmosphere for fun for those employees who work under your leadership:

1. <u>There is a big difference between fun and funny.</u>
Most resistance to the notion of humor in the workplace stems from the failure to recognize the distinction between having fun and being funny. Whenever humor is mentioned, we reflexively think of jokes and laughter, behaviors usually associated with being funny. Although the two concepts sometimes overlap, fun has little to do with funny.

Funny is a behavior designed to provoke laughter. As we've already observed, funny needs laughter to be successful. Being funny is not always possible, nor is it always appropriate.

Fun has no need of laughter. Viewing a beautiful sunset, hearing a rapturous symphony, or receiving a compliment from someone who loves you can all be fun, without stirring even a snicker. Fun is measured more by the level of enjoyment, not by the intensity of a laugh. This distinction may be critical in a business atmosphere.

Some shoppers go out of their way to find bargains. My wife, Connie, goes out of her way for a smile.

There are two different supermarket chains in our vicinity. In one, the checkout people just go through the motions. They exhibit no enthusiasm and make no eye contact with the customer. If they talk at all, it is to one another about matters not pertaining to the work they are doing.

In the other store, the employees are smiling and cheerful. They greet each customer personally and make pleasant conversation while they ring up the goods. You get the feeling they are enjoying their jobs.

Both supermarkets are the same size (major chains) and, in both, the employees are the same age range. The only difference, aside from the Fun Factor differential, is that the second market is about a mile further from our house than the first.

Nevertheless, Connie happily goes the extra mile for the extra smiles.

Fun is nothing but pure energy, supported by an attitude. Having fun is always possible and it's always appropriate. If you say you do not want more fun in your workplace, you are really saying you do not want more energy in your business. I don't think that's what you mean.

So, let's be clear about our intentions. Unless your business happens to be a comedy club or amusement park, more laughter is not the goal. I am not suggesting that you entertain your employees with comedy or that you teach them to be comedians. I am simply advocating that you endorse fun as the energy upon which your company runs and that you do what you can to create a corporate culture that allows and encourages it.

Which leads to the second thing to remember:

2. <u>You must choose whether to lead by fear or by fun.</u>
Creating an atmosphere of fun is all about leadership. The person at the top has to set the tone and this responsibility cannot be delegated. If you want the benefits of the Fun Factor for your

company, you must take the initiative to call it forth.

Your effectiveness as a leader is dependent on one factor above all. There is an essential element that must always be in the mix, without which a leader cannot be successful. That element is not vision, charisma, passion, or communication skills, as important as those qualities may be. The one essential element is .. followers. Every leader needs followers. If you can't get people to follow you, you shouldn't call yourself a leader.

Think about what happens when a person attempts to inspire and motivate others to behave in certain ways. There are only three general responses possible and two of them are not good. First there is indifference. Indifference is the least desirable response for any would-be leader. If people are unmoved and apathetic towards your attempts to call them forth, if you can't even make a "dent" in their inertia, about the only thing you can do is pray for divine intervention.

Second, there is resistance. Resistance is usually not a welcome sight to a would-be leader, but at least it's better than no response at all. You know you're getting a reaction, even if it's not the one you want. There is something to work with, a "foot in the door." It may be an uphill battle but perhaps, over time, you can learn the reasons for the resistance and do something about it. At least there's more hope here than with indifference.

Third, there is acceptance. Acceptance is the response a would-be leader is looking for. However, just because they've accepted you as their leader, it doesn't mean you're home free. Acceptance itself comes in three varieties—compliance, cooperation and collaboration.

Compliance is the least desirable of these three. Many leaders are satisfied with compliance in their followers, but, if you are looking to be truly successful, you should hope for better. Compliance is nothing more than willingness to follow the leader's instructions. It implies no enthusiasm or endorsement on the part of the follower. The motivating element is usually the power and authority attributed to the leader. As such, compliance tends to be fear-based.

As in a fear-based family, when compliant followers ask

"Why?" the leader says, "Because I said so." We already know that fear can motivate, but we have observed that fear-based behavior is difficult to sustain in family life. The same holds true for the workplace.

Cooperation is an improvement upon compliance. When followers cooperate with their leaders, they are bringing some of their own energy to the table. Cooperation is a limited endorsement of the leader's goal. The limitation is that the leader sets and owns the goals. When the follower cooperates, he is actively helping to achieve the leader's objectives. In cooperation, the follower says to the leader, "I think your goal is a worthy one and I will work hard to help you achieve it."

There is less fear and more fun in cooperation than compliance, though the fun is limited to the altruistic satisfaction of helping another person achieve his or her goals. In that sense we might consider it vicarious fun. Although many leaders are quite pleased when they get cooperation, I think it's possible to do even better.

Collaboration is the best form of acceptance, because, for the follower, it involves more than just following orders, and it also goes beyond the contribution of some independent effort. Collaboration occurs when followers embrace and adopt a leader's objectives, as though they were their own. True collaboration is akin to a partnership, with leader and follower both "owning" the vision and having a stake in the outcome. It asks for and achieves mutuality between leader and followers—mutuality of effort and mutuality of satisfaction. If something should deter the leader, the collaborator will be prepared to carry on independently, because he is doing it as much for himself as for the other person. The prevailing energy of collaboration is fun, not fear.

If you want maximum success with your business, make collaborators of your employees. The best way to accomplish this goal is to create an atmosphere of fun and participate in it with them. This is a conscious choice, not something to be left up to chance.

This brings us to the third thing to remember.

3. <u>You must serve as a personal example of the Fun Factor.</u>
What we observe in many examples of fearless, fun-filled family life holds equally true for the workplace. You cannot create a fun environment by fiat. You have to show up and be involved. That means you must be having fun yourself before you can successfully share that energy with others. Put another way, if you draw mostly on fear to motivate yourself, you will be unable to avoid fear-based leadership tactics.

Creating an environment of fun is not a quick fix, nor can it be done overnight. Don't expect it to happen by arranging a weekend offsite teambuilding event, although that can be an important part of a long-term process. One-shot bonding events have limited value because they are so brief and usually occur out of the mainstream of the work setting. The sustainable atmosphere of fun you seek gives energy to and draws energy from the context of real work.

This requires showing up every day with credible strategies and skills that reinforce the emphasis of fun over fear. If you do not truly believe that having fun is essential for your personal best effort, you're likely to fall into the same trap as the parent who says "Do as I say, not as I do." Your employees will pay more attention to your behavior than your words. If you are not "walking your talk" about having fun, they'll assume it's just another gimmick to get more work out of them.

Bob, a hospital social worker, attended my workshop in Portland, Oregon. Hearing of the work I do with Jerry Lewis, he wanted to share the following anecdote.

As it turned out, social work was a second career for Bob. In his "first life" he had been a musician. He recalled that about twenty years ago, he was a member of the house orchestra of a major Las Vegas showroom, when Jerry Lewis came in for a two-week engagement.

"The first day of rehearsals, Mr. Lewis wanted to meet everybody in the band," Bob recounted. "He asked us where we were from and wanted to know about our wives and our kids. He took a personal interest in each of us."

Bob continued. "Here's what impressed me. He must have memorized all the information, because for the rest of the two week run, he greeted everybody by name, asked about our wives and kids by name, and made mention of specific details he had learned about us. It made us feel that we were important to him, and I'll tell you, there wasn't anything we wouldn't have gladly done in return to make his show a success."

"It's been twenty years," he concluded, "and I have never forgotten it. It was one of the best experiences I had in show business."

I am convinced that nobody enjoys being manipulated. Yes, we may be willing to make occasional exceptions for magicians, illusionists, stage hypnotists and mystery writers, if the situation is right. Even then, we usually see ourselves as "volunteering" to suspend our disbelief, for purposes of our amusement. Rarely are we happy when someone usurps our right to decide for ourselves.

You will find this especially true if you are hoping to encourage other people to have fun. You can't manipulate them into it. Remember my comedy mentor's distinction between "making them laugh" and "sharing a laugh with them." If you are trying too hard to make them laugh, the effort becomes apparent and employees will resent it, and resist it.

What we're talking about here is honest communication and trust, elements that are second nature to a fearless family. Employees, like children in a family, must trust that you will not humiliate, embarrass, or exploit them, when they allow themselves to have fun. You as the leader, like a parent in a family, must similarly trust that employees will not abuse the opportunity to have fun by becoming disrespectful or otherwise undermining the discipline necessary to meet important objectives. As in family life, there is mutual vulnerability here.

One measure that you are being "honest" with your employees is the intensity of your passion. You can't fake passion. Your passion will spread to your employees. It will be inspiring and infectious. Once you set passion loose in the workplace, you will be amazed at the results.

Cheap Joe's Art Stuff, located in Boone, North Carolina, has grown in less than 20 years from occupying one shelf in the Boone Drug Store in 1984 to its current status as a worldwide distributor of art supplies with more than 60 full-time employees. In a recent interview, I asked owner Joe Miller what he felt was responsible for the success of his business.

A renowned artist himself, he answered, "I've learned that talent is not the thing it's cracked up to be. I believe we all have about the same amount of talent. The big thing is passion. Desire."

When I asked him what it was like to work at "Cheap Joe's," Miller referred me to his employees. Here's a sampling of their responses:

"The business is run like a family; everyone is treated with respect and rewarded for their efforts ... I've never been welcomed so warmly to a company before."

"The esprit de corps here is unequalled at any workplace I've experienced. The love and good will I feel when I walk through that door each morning staggers me more often than not."

"There are signs at the entrance greeting special guests and friends." (I experienced this personally when I arrived for my visit.)

"Joe loves all his employees."

"Joe says something kind to every employee, smiles a lot and gives out hugs to everyone who needs one."

"There is a sense of community and family. It's the way everyone is so helpful to one another ... Cheap Joe's also cares about the community and works to help the less fortunate."

Joe Miller added a fitting summary to his business philosophy. "You have to love what you're doing, and if you let yourself go with that current, everything else will work out."

Building social capital is another way to understand the effects you get from unleashing fun in the workplace. In their book, *Good Company* (2001), Cohen and Prusak define the term social capital as the "stock of active connections among people: the trust, mutual understanding, and shared values and behaviors that bind the members of human networks and communities and make cooperative action possible." This reminds me of a fearless, fun-filled family.

The authors go on to say, "Social capital makes an organization, or any cooperative group, more than a collection of individuals intent on achieving their own private purposes. Social capital bridges the space between people. Its characteristic elements and indicators include high levels of trust, robust personal networks and vibrant communities, shared understandings, and a sense of equitable participation in a joint enterprise—all things that draw individuals together into a group." To me, this sounds like the grown up version of a playground.

If you truly believe that your humor nature is your most trustworthy and reliable personal asset for success, then you will already be practicing certain techniques or strategies for your own benefit. In the previous chapter, we reviewed a few of them that you found personally helpful—smiling more often, looking for the pony, letting go frequently, keeping it fresh and making up games. Before considering corporate strategies, make sure your personal strategies are strong and in place. Be willing to trust yourself. If you are having fun, employees will be unable to resist the invitation to join you.

Here are some leadership strategies that strengthen and sustain a fun atmosphere:

1. <u>Listen Very Carefully</u>

If you didn't feel that people were your company's strongest and most valuable asset, you probably wouldn't have read this far. So, how do you communicate this to every person in your working environment? You put it into action by taking the time to listen to them.

Any leader who seeks the benefits of the Fun Factor would be well advised to follow Stephen Covey's advice that it is more important to seek to understand than to be understood. If we are talking about true collaboration, it must be based on a mutual sharing of purpose and goals. You might begin by asking your employees the questions we recommended in the last chapter, questions that every individual should ideally be asking of himself. Ask them why they have chosen the work that they do for you. What or who influenced them? What do they expect to accomplish that will meet their needs for self-fulfillment? How do they define success?

It's not enough to ask these questions. You must take the time to listen to the answers you get. The time you spend listening will be your most valuable investment in the social capital of your company.

What has this got to do with fun? Just this. Being listened to and understood is the most fun a humor being can ever have. It is not surprising that the number one reason people give for leaving their jobs is not the salary, the hours, or the physical work. It is that they do not feel appreciated. America's workers do not feel that they count as individuals. Employees who are listened to feel valued, appreciated and supported.

Not to mention the fact that, if you listen carefully, you will be given the game plan for making your workplace more fun. Employees will tell you what turns them on. Unless you're in the habit of rolling up your sleeves and periodically pinch-hitting for your workers, you may have a surprise or two coming. They know their jobs better than you.

If you give them the opportunity and are willing to back them up, your employees will revolutionize your working environment. And, when you start implementing their suggestions, or, better yet, giving them the green light to make the changes themselves, that's when the fun really begins. That's when the collaboration becomes real. Employees will have a greater stake in a successful outcome if it's their own plan they are working with.

2. Stay focused, but remain flexible.

This strategy is complementary to the listening strategy. The Fun Factor will not be supported by a closed mind. If you already know all the answers, don't make a pretense of asking the questions. You must be willing to be influenced by what you hear and see. Mutuality requires flexibility.

On the other hand, somebody has to keep the overall destination in focus, and that's you. The flexibility required for fun doesn't ask that you abandon your game plan, just that you be willing to consider more than one way to achieve it. If it's "my way or the highway," you might get the product out, but it won't be much fun and sustaining the effort will be a problem.

If you have followed the plan thus far, you have already demonstrated the kind of flexibility we're talking about. We have agreed that increased customer satisfaction is and should be the overriding goal in any successful business. A direct path to that objective would have been to establish and reinforce the principle that "the customer is always right." Yet, by being willing to put your employees first, you have accepted a more "indirect" route to that same goal. In striving for greater employee satisfaction you know that, even if it involves momentarily putting your customer in second place, you will ultimately insure your primary objective.

John, a bank president, was recalling a lesson taught to him by his mentor, the former president of his bank.

"One day he watched me handling a customer complaint and drew me aside afterwards. He asked me why I had corrected our employee in front of the customer, instead of privately.

I told him I had done it that way to make a point.

'And what point were you making?" he asked.

I explained, 'I wanted the employee and the customer both to get the message that in this bank the customer is always right, regardless of the particulars.'

He smiled and put his arm around my shoulder. 'I'd rather we go by the principle that the customer is always <u>satisfied</u>, regardless of the particulars. As to who's right, I think we should always assume it's our employee, until proven otherwise. Let's work on satisfying our customers without undermining our employees.'

He made a valuable distinction for me that I have never forgotten."

3. <u>Be willing to laugh at yourself.</u>

As the boss, the very best instrument you have for initiating an atmosphere of fun is yourself. So, take advantage of every opportunity to laugh at your own silliness. Willingness to take yourself less seriously will not only provide you with more personal fun, it will also encourage your employees to view themselves from the same perspective.

Often leaders fear that their followers will respect them less, if they share self-deprecating humor. In reality, it is usually quite the opposite. Most people will view your willingness to laugh at yourself as a sign of strength, an admirable trait. They will gain, not lose, respect.

One morning, during our clinic staff meeting, I was reading out loud a letter I had received from a patient who was unhappy with the service I had provided during a recent appointment. As the clinic director, I thought it would be instructive for all of the staff to discuss the patient's complaints and brainstorm with me on how to improve my service next time.

I reached a particularly angry sentence in the letter, which read, "Dr. Kuhn, let us suppose for a moment you are not God ..." As I read this aloud, I sensed a sudden tension in the room. After all, I was the boss. How dare she address me in such sarcastic tones?

I looked up from the paper into the stunned faces of the residents, nurses and staff members sitting around the table.

Then I said, "OK—but only for a moment!"

Everyone laughed, and as we did, the tension disappeared and we were able to learn from my mistakes.

4. Keep expecting the unexpected.

We discussed the role of frequent surprises in spicing up fun-filled family life.

They will have the same effect in the workplace environment. To allow for, and even invite, surprises into the mix, you might need to "unlearn" what you think you know about the unexpected in life, especially if you were not raised in a fearless family.

Commonly the emergence of an unexpected turn of events is viewed as evidence of poor preparation or lack of competence. The CEO who demands, "I don't want any surprises," is really asking for a high level of competence. Yet, we have found that the most competent people, recognizing that unexpected and uncalled-for occurrences are inevitable, seem able to turn them to their advantage.

In their book, *The Hardy Executive: Health Under Stress* (1985), Maddi and Kobasa reported on their landmark study of some of America's top executives. They were interested in learning the most consistent traits shared by those leaders who exhibited the greatest resilience in the face of stress. The most "stress hardy" executives in their study all shared the capacity to embrace unexpected occurrences as opportunities, not setbacks. These executives seemed to reflexively "welcome" surprises and even to seek them out as a stimulus to growth and creativity. As you have probably guessed, "stress hardiness" was highly correlated with both success and good health.

The unexpected is the lifeblood of humor and fun. By welcoming it as a potential asset in your business environment, you are inviting everyone in the company to have more fun. Your personal tolerance for surprises will be the standard by which your intentions will be measured.

When Jerry Lewis and I began developing our "Laughter and Healing" seminar, I told him I was frankly surprised at the many literary references he drew upon, since it was well known that he lacked a formal education.

He laughed. "I'm happy to surprise you," he said. "I think surprises are good. I wake up every morning praying for at least one surprise sometime during the day."

5. Welcome mistakes

This is a tough one. Welcoming mistakes can be misconstrued as endorsing incompetence. This strategy is not meant to provide a license for ineptitude. It is designed to dismantle the fears that limit performance.

Professional speaker Steve Allen, Jr., MD, teaches juggling in his workshops as a means of relieving stress. In order to ensure that his audiences will have fun learning to juggle, he always starts his lessons the same way.

"The first thing I want you to practice is how to drop things successfully," he instructs. He then leads everyone in a ritual of gleefully and "artfully" dropping the material they are going to be juggling.

Steve believes that, getting the "fear" of dropping things out of the way right from the start, frees people to have more fun with their juggling efforts.

Dr. Allen has given us yet another example of the antagonistic relationship between fun and fear. If we remove fear, more fun is inevitable. If your employees are afraid of making a mistake, they will not be having much fun. Instead of playing to win, they will be playing not to lose. Think back to the last time you witnessed a sporting event in which one team was playing not to lose. Do you remember how tentatively and conservatively it played? I'll bet there was no spontaneity, confidence or joy in evidence. Is this how you want your workforce to perform?

As with many strategies that support the Fun Factor, this one demands more than lip service. When you invite your employees to take the "risk" of letting their humor natures prevail, you must be prepared to back it up with action. Mistakes will be made. If they are not tolerated, the spirit of fun will be crushed.

Southwest Airlines has received a great deal of recognition for their success in creating and maintaining a corporate culture that encourages employees to have fun on the job. Their well-documented results in terms of high employee morale, low personnel turnover, and profitability are clear examples of the benefits of this strategy, at a time when those kinds of statistics have been hard to come by in their industry.

I have interviewed many of their employees. They are a happy, satisfied lot. Comments such as: "This is the best company I've ever worked for" and "I used to be with (a competitor). I wouldn't go back to them for twice the money!" are the rule, not the exception. I believe that one of the most crucial elements of Southwest Airline's culture is their willingness to support employees whenever they try new ways to have fun and it doesn't work out. Understandably they do not put up with patterns of repeated incompetence, but if an "honest" mistake is made, no one is hung out to dry.

That's loyalty that works both ways.

6. Act and interact

This strategy has to do with tangible evidence of your intentions.

Good ideas are of little more than passing interest, unless they are put into practice. For example, it's true that people find it fun to be listened to. But if, after soliciting their ideas and thoughts, you provide no evidence that they will influence your actions, your employees will begin to distrust you.

Nothing stimulates the Fun Factor more than these three words: "Let's try it." And that means really trying, not just making a token effort.

Seinfeld, the television show, was a disaster in its first season. At that time it was named *The Seinfeld Chronicles*, and if it hadn't been for the perseverance of one executive at NBC who thought he saw some potential in it, the show would have been consigned for eternity to the scrap heap. Instead, it survived, ran for eight seasons and won multiple Emmys.

Also, social interactions are important components of an atmosphere of fun. For the most part these activities will take place outside the workplace. A company softball or bowling team draws the participation of employees with common interests. Special events, such as movies, dinners, or museum trips encourage the inclusion of spouses and other family members in the fun.

The goal is to provide formal and informal "extra curricular" activities, so that employees learn more about each other and have the opportunity to form strong bonds of friendship. It certainly is more fun going to work when you know and like the people on your team.

7. Build in relevance to the larger community.

Fun-based companies find ways to give back to the communities from which they draw their support. This is a "selfish" habit that makes good business sense and provides employees with additional opportunities for fun.

Making a difference plays a large part in having fun at work. If a person sees his job only as a vehicle by which the company makes a profit, he will be hard pressed to have fun. If the company is making an identifiable difference in the community in which it resides, meaning is added to the work. When work has added meaning it becomes more fun for the workers.

When it comes to what your company stands for, it is important for you, as the leader, to have clearly in mind your answers to those fundamental questions we asked earlier. Why do you do the work you do? What personal priorities are served by your success? How does your work fit into the larger picture of your life? Are you motivated by fear or fun? What purpose is served by your success?

The personal values unearthed by these questions are the values that you will communicate to your company. The company's values will ultimately reflect your own. What <u>does</u> your company stand for? Assuming you skillfully and efficiently make an excellent product, you and your employees can justifiably take pride in that. But, how do you see your product and your company contributing to the common good? Are you a company that makes a great product or a great company that "uses" its success to make a difference in the world? Both descriptions may be true, but the second goes much farther than the first.

As you examine the answers to these questions, you are articulating your company's relevance to the community in which it exists. This is important to a corporate atmosphere of fun because relevance and meaning provide satisfaction and pride to your personnel. By calling on your employees to look beyond the confines of their individual jobs and consider the opportunities they have to make their community a better place, you are inspiring them to be better citizens, while giving them yet another reason to enjoy being a part of your organization.

As they take on projects together, employees will discover that they can have more impact as a group than separately. You will want to set the stage for such activity and make appropriate resources available, but I encourage you to let your employees in on the fun early in the process. Establish an employee task force to help you identify community needs and organize your corporate responses. Local, hands-on projects are preferable to grand gestures supporting more generic causes, simply because they have a more immediate and personal impact on your company personnel. Most important of all, be sure you show up to do your share of the work involved in carrying out the projects. It's a great opportunity for you to "walk your talk."

Whether it is building a house for Habitat for Humanity, cleaning up a local park, or raising money for Jerry's Kids, this kind of activity gives employees a strong identity with your company and an element of pride in what it stands for. They can enjoy wearing the company logo both inside and outside the workplace.

8. Celebrate everything.

Constant celebrating breeds joy, which is just another name for the energy of fun. Ironically, in an atmosphere of fun, everything is cause for celebration. Does this mean that the workplace should become a never-ending party? It depends on what you mean by party.

Here's another fun-based concept that is easy to reject, if we remain trapped in our old trivializing thoughts about humor. Celebration can be of at least two types. Yes, there is indeed what we will call the noisy type, replete with balloons, decorations, noisemakers, and fireworks. New Year's Eve and the Fourth of July are perfect examples. These events are what we usually think about the instant the word celebration is mentioned.

There is nothing wrong with noisy celebrations, except that they usually require certain qualifications, like a designated holiday, general public acceptance (you can't go shooting off fireworks just any old time), and some expenditure of effort planning in advance and cleaning up afterwards. I say take advantage of every opportunity you get to enjoy that kind of celebration. It's fun.

There is another type of celebration that is a bit more feasible on a day-to-day basis. We will call it quiet celebration. It involves the more subtle recognition of the many good things in our lives that usually go unnoticed. Does this sound familiar? It should. It is simply an extension of our fun strategy—Look for the Pony.

Quiet celebrations are always possible. They are a product

of the willingness to explicitly profess gratitude for something or someone we would otherwise implicitly take for granted. Practicing this kind of celebration cultivates gratitude. If it becomes a daily habit, it produces an attitude of sensitivity and respect for every good thing. When that attitude pervades a workplace, it results in a constant appreciation of the people involved, for who they are as well as what they do.

Ken Blanchard, the co-author of the book, *The One Minute Manager*, has written, "Of all the concepts I have taught managers over the years, the most important has been the power of praising." Every celebration is a chance to publicly say thank you to someone. Successful leaders of fun-filled companies do not let these opportunities get past them. They become effective in what Blanchard calls "catching somebody in the act of doing something right."

Quiet celebration doesn't require a designated holiday and certainly doesn't need fireworks. To succeed, it must be timely, sincere and personal. It also must be public whenever possible. Making this kind of recognition privately wastes much of its benefit for your workplace environment. When we witness our colleague receiving praise and recognition, we identify with her, and to a certain extent, feel better about ourselves. But, it doesn't stop there. We also are gratified to know that somebody is paying attention to what we do. This adds significance to our work and gives us added incentive to do our best.

Another common mistake that undermines the benefits of frequent celebration is delegating the responsibility. This will not work. Once again, as in so many of the strategies we've looked at, you can't phone it in. You, as the boss, must be involved personally in the celebration rituals. If employee celebrations are not important enough to make a dent in your schedule, you might want to rethink your motivation for creating a fun environment in the first place.

I was invited to give the keynote address for the annual meeting of a national corporation. An audience of 200 managers and supervisors applauded as the CEO stood before them to introduce me. In his introduction, he lauded my work with humor and gave his personal endorsement to the idea of having more fun in their corporate setting.

He shook my hand as I arrived at the podium, promptly left the room, and did not return. As he disappeared from sight, so did the enthusiasm of the audience. The energy drop was palpable. He might as well have said the words, "Now, if you'll excuse me, you are not important enough for me to join you in having fun," because that's the message everyone received.

Oh, we had some fun that morning, the managers and I. But there was nothing I could do to restore the level of enthusiasm the CEO sucked out of the room when he left. I offered to bring it to his attention afterward, but the person who invited me thought it would be better if I didn't. The sad thing is, he will probably never know what he's missing.

The concept of constant celebration ends this chapter, and, at the same time, provides a prelude to the next. We are ready now to examine some examples of how humor strategies look and sound as they play out in the everyday life of organizations and become part of the company culture. Sustaining the Fun Factor is the focus of the chapter that follows. As you read on, I'm sure you will notice that there is a strong element of celebration in nearly every example.

Chapter Seven

REWARDING AND REINFORCING THE FUN FACTOR AT WORK

In the previous chapter, inspired by Joseph Manckiewicz' advice, "Create an atmosphere for fun, and you'll get great work," we discussed the process of establishing an atmosphere of fun in your workplace. Now we turn our attention to the means by which the Fun Factor is maintained and sustained on a day-to-day basis.

Having recruited your colleagues and personnel to acts of daily celebration, the challenge now is how to keep them at it. That can be tricky. Fun-based motivation can turn to fear-based in the twinkling of an eye.

Example I.

A company hired a consultant to help it increase its efficiency. After a thorough study, the consultant recommended two major initiatives. First, was the elimination of one third of the personnel, along with a restructuring of job descriptions to more efficiently run the business – downsizing. The second was an incentive campaign to eliminate waste, whereby each employee was invited to actively identify wasteful practices in the workplace and bring them to the attention of management. The deal was that if, by eliminating the wasteful practice, the company saved money, the employee who reported it would share in the savings by way of a financial reward.

Initially the employee response was enthusiastic and exuberant. The idea of "running a tighter ship" appealed to everyone. Morale picked up, and personnel embraced the incentive plan as a long-overdue process. Everyone was inspired to identify ways to save costs and, since things had been so inefficient for so long, there was no lack of opportunity. The ideas and the cash rewards were abundant. An atmosphere of fun had emerged.

This lasted for about six months, by which time most of the downsizing had been accomplished and most of the easy-to-identify inefficiencies had been spotted, reported and eliminated. It began to dawn on the employees that the efficiency of downsizing was going to mean more work with fewer resources for those who remained employed. Also, with respect to the incentive plan for identifying cost-savings, once all the fruit had been picked from the lower, easily accessible, branches of the tree, what remained was available only to those with ladders. The few "plums" that remained accessible to the rank and file, spawned hot debate over "who spotted them first." Reward bonuses had become a rarity.

The situation quickly deteriorated into competitive bickering, turf guarding and accusations of deception. Resentment was rampant among the employees, who felt they had been manipulated and exploited. Morale plummeted. If anything, it was worse than before the initiatives were begun.

Management, on the other hand, felt unappreciated after all the effort it had put into making the company stronger. They accused the rank and file of being "spoiled" by all the bonuses, and resented their "what have you done for us lately" attitude. They regretted ever having instituted the incentive program.

The workplace had become a fear-based environment.

Contrast this story with the following account:

Example II.

In the mid-1990s a textile factory, in the midst of a troubled industry, was completely destroyed by fire. The retirement-age CEO made a decision that stunned the business world and turned him into a hero.

The CEO was Aaron Feuerstein. The textile factory was Malden Mills. The destructive fire could easily have resulted in the unemployment of 3000 people. However, Mr. Feuerstein decided to keep everyone on the payroll until a new factory could be built.

Both of these stories are true. The second is a rare instance. The first is unfortunately an all-too-common occurrence.

What was the problem in the first Example? The company seemed to have turned a corner in creating renewed enthusiasm in the workforce. What made the wheels fall off after only six months? As a generalization, it seems that the company fell into what Dr. Barry Heermann calls "an obsessive preoccupation with organizational form and structure and with mechanisms intended to raise efficiencies." Writing in the book, *The New Bottom Line: Bringing Heart and Soul to Business* (edited by Renesch and Defoore, New Leaders Press, 1996), he identifies this preoccupation as a major "inhibitor of organizational effectiveness" in corporate America today. Dr. Heermann goes on to write:

"… In modern business there are a great many ways to get busy while getting nowhere. Here are some of the painfully familiar dysfunctional practices that I have observed in my work with organizations:

· adopt new and imaginative job restructuring and job titles for employees, but do nothing to address the fact that they still bring old, unchallenged assumptions to their work.

· escalate the rhetoric of customer service, without coming to terms with what customers are looking for or how to provide greater service.

· design a nonhierarchical organization chart, while everyone working there still knows who disposes of the power, and who is disposable.

· establish a new strategic planning process without involving the individuals who are responsible for achieving the result.

· introduce a highly-touted product improvement that does nothing to dispel long-standing customer complaints.

"In each case, the company claimed—perhaps it even believed—that answers had been found to lead it to team and organizational success. Unfortunately, events proved otherwise. Instead of freeing team spirit or achieving efficiencies, these changes mired employees further, diminishing their sense of self-worth and trivializing their work."

Although our hapless company didn't commit all of these errors, there are some that appear to apply. Certainly Dr. Heermann's description of the disappointing outcome rings true. Let's take a closer look.

In the first place, the company failed to recognize that eliminating waste, as helpful as that may be at times, is in reality a fear-based strategy. Don't get me wrong. I think we should all strive to be as efficient as possible. But, I want to point out that, by its very nature, this is a very limited game plan for success. Like all strategies inspired by the fear factor, eliminating waste involves "playing not to lose."

To illustrate, let's imagine two fictional companies in competition with each other. Both discover that through certain inefficiencies they are losing 25 cents on every dollar earned. Company A decides on a strategy to eliminate waste. It has immediately placed a limit on its success, for two reasons. First, it will never be able to eliminate all the inefficiencies. All it will do is minimize them. Second, even if it comes close to perfection in its campaign, at its best it will only be capturing 100 percent of each dollar it started with.

Company B decides on a different plan. It urges its employees to continue to try new things and to take reasonable risks, in an effort to expand product lines and sales opportunities. It essentially ignores the inefficiencies that are "built in" to this approach and reassures its employees that "waste" will be tolerated if it results from efforts to be innovative. This strategy produces a doubling of sales, creating two dollars of income for every one it started with.

Now, both companies have been successful. Company A, with its newfound efficiency, has increased its profits by 33 percent ($.75 to $1.00). However, Company B, despite its continued inefficiencies, enjoys a 100 percent increase ($.75 to $1.50). If they are indeed competing for the same customers, in which of these two companies would you rather own stock?

The company in Example I put itself in the same position as Company A. The fear basis of its strategy took six months to come to light, but it was there from the beginning. So, our first lesson is that not everything that promises to be fun ends up that way.

Another mistake made by the unsuccessful company is that it failed to realize the mixed message it was sending to its personnel. When it announced its intention to "downsize" at the same time it was launching a campaign to eliminate waste, employees were likely to have heard that becoming more efficient might cost them their jobs. In other words, efficiency appeared to be more important than people. When personnel hear this message, it pretty much takes the fun out of coming to work. So, the big incentive plan had a powerful disincentive built into it. Lesson number two: If you want an atmosphere of fun to last, make sure you don't have hidden disincentives for the behaviors you are trying to encourage.

A third flaw in the company's plan could have been that the waste elimination campaign inadvertently encouraged employees to catch one another doing "something wrong." This is in direct contrast to Ken Blanchard's concept of catching someone in the "act of doing something right," which we mentioned in the last chapter. It can lead to an atmosphere of apprehension and guardedness, divisive sentiments that only serve to enhance the fear factor, while diminishing the fun. Lesson number three: If you want a sustainable atmosphere for fun, it pays to emphasize the positives, not the negatives.

This leads to the fourth mistake, perhaps the most common of all among companies that fail in their attempts to create a fun environment. The strategy ultimately produced increased competition among the personnel. At first, this wasn't apparent because there were enough examples of waste to make everybody a "winner." But once the low-hanging fruit was picked, competition set in for the fewer prizes that remained. This set up rivalries and tensions that were not conducive to an atmosphere of fun. So, the fourth lesson to be drawn from this example is that sustainable fun is in jeopardy when internal competition is inflamed.

By looking carefully at the experience of the company in Example I, we have identified some potential pitfalls that caused fear to erode an earnest attempt to create a fun environment. Before we go on to discuss ways to avoid these pitfalls, let's look at the company in Example II. How does it measure up against these potential "traps?"

By his decision to keep every employee on the payroll throughout the crisis, Mr. Feuerstein eliminated fear, sent an unmistakably positive message, obviated the need for turf-guarding and in-fighting and guaranteed winners all around. He could not have made a better investment in the future of his company. In contrast to Example I, Example II has a happier outcome because the company sent a clear message that people were more important than anything else.

However, neither story is conclusive because in both instances the most important question remains unanswered, namely how did the company follow up its attempt to tap into the Fun Factor? Follow-up and maintenance is the real challenge. Although it may not be easy to create an atmosphere of fun, it's duck soup when compared to sustaining it.

It all goes back to a basic principle we learned early in this book Fun comes from within and works its way out. The HA HA HA prescription is every bit as important to a company as it is to the individual and the family. Attitude creates atmosphere, which then results in action. Action is the culminating, not the initiating, event. That is why in the last chapter we spent so much time asking about attitudes and values. Sustainable fun requires more than window dressing. It requires a corporate culture built on an attitude of trusting the humor nature of everyone involved, starting with your own.

According to Freiberg and Freiberg, culture is the "glue that holds our organizations together." As these authors explain in their best-selling book, *Nuts!*, corporate culture "encompasses beliefs, expectations, norms, rituals, communication patterns, symbols, heroes, and reward structures. Culture is not about magic formulas and secret plans; it is a combination of a thousand things."

Your corporate culture is the heart of your company, reflecting your values and priorities. Herb Kelleher, founder of Southwest Airlines, puts it this way: "Culture is one of the most precious things a company has, so you must work harder at it than anything else." A sustainable atmosphere of fun must come from the heart of a company. Conspicuous fun-filled events are the product of an atmosphere for fun, not the cause.

So when we talk about reinforcing the Fun Factor in a company environment, we are talking more about basic values than specific techniques. As when we discussed rewarding and reinforcing the Fun Factor in the family (Chapter Four), those charged with the responsibilities of leadership must be truly willing to openly share power and information in a collaborative effort. Trust and open communication go hand in hand in a fearless environment.

Two companies that have in recent years been lauded as outstanding examples of value-led businesses are Ben & Jerry's Homemade, Inc. and Southwest Airlines. Not surprisingly, they both are also well recognized for their success in building the Fun Factor into their corporate cultures. Each has published its list of core values.

First, here are Ben & Jerry's List of "Aspirations":

1. To Be Real: We need to be who we say we are …
2. To Be the Best: Our future together depends upon our ability to outperform the competition …
3. To Improve Continuously: … we are responsible for helping to shape and improve what goes on around us.
4. To Learn Continuously: We'll need to keep growing skills in three areas: technical skills, personal skills, and business knowledge.
5. To Be Inclusive: We embrace individual differences …
6. To Be Creative: Our creativity is our strength …
7. To Build Community: When one of us needs help, we reach out

to help …
8. To Be Open and Trusting: We need to make sure people feel safe to speak up about things they care about …
9. To Celebrate and Give Meaningful Recognition: … We should make recognition a contagious part of everyday life.
10. To Use Consultive Decision Making and Active Listening: … we must be active listeners.
11. To Hold Ourselves Accountable: When we don't do our part it affects everybody …
12. To Be Great Communicators: Good leaders have well-informed teams …
13. To Be Up-Front: Good straight feedback is essential to improvement …
14. To Be Profitable by Being Thrifty: We believe in investing wisely and with a sense of frugality …
(Cohen and Greefield, *Ben & Jerry's Double-Dip*, Fireside, 1998)

In case you're thinking those values come easily only because they are making a product (ice cream) that is associated with fun, see how they compare to those of a company that takes thousands of people into the air every day. Here are Southwest Airlines' core values, followed by their list of Values in Action:

1. Profitability: … drives the company's growth and is directly linked to profit-sharing and to job security …
2. Low Cost: … employees continually look for ways to save money without sacrificing service.
3. Family: … when you treat employees like family, you foster the kind of intimacy and informality that builds strong relationships and makes work more fun.
4. Fun: The company is serious about creating an environment where play, humor, creativity, and laughter flourish …
5. Love: Employees are expected to care about people and act in ways that affirm their dignity and worth …
6. Hard Work: The pace at Southwest Airlines is fast and intense

7. Individuality: When people are free to be themselves, they are liberated to express their true gifts and talents ...

8. Ownership: ... people take better care of things they own ...

9. Legendary Service: ... happy, satisfied customers who return again and again create job security ...

10. Egalitarianism: ... executives are expected to do the things they ask others to do ...

11. Common Sense/Good Judgment: ... The company wants people who think "service" before adherence to rules.

12. Simplicity: ... simplicity creates speed, reduces costs, and fosters understanding ...

13. Altruism: ... there is a tremendous sense of joy and satisfaction that comes from helping others.

Values in Action:

1. Be Visionary: Vision is the bigger picture that motivates employees

2. Celebrate Everything: Southwest throws a party whenever possible to honor and reward people ...

3. Hire the Right People: ... The company is famous for hiring people who are not afraid to express their individuality, take risks, and assume responsibility ...

4. Limit Committees and Keep Them Ad Hoc: The use of committees in general is not favored ...

5. Keep a Warrior Spirit: ... if you're going to do something, do it with intensity and do it right.

6. Keep Multiple Scenarios: ... forecast and plan by preparing for a variety of possibilities.

7. Minimize Paperwork: ... Don't type a memo – just get it done.

8. Feel Free to be Informal: ... Casual wear facilitates and encourages the playful creative spirit at work within the company

9. Move Fast: Getting things done and having a bias for action are norms ...

10. Dare to be Different: Southwest employees think like mavericks (Freiberg and Freiberg, *Nuts!*, Bard Press, 1996)

Although these two companies do very different things, they have much in common. In both there is a decided emphasis on creating a sense of family, that fosters mutual respect, mutual trust, mutual risk and mutual caring – a fearless, fun-filled family, if you will. Each encourages open dialogue among all levels of personnel and "unselfishly" celebrates individual incentive and achievements. Neither sees any conflict between the serious goals of hard work and accountability and the lighthearted ones of fun and celebration. Finally both encourage corporate efforts to make a difference in the world beyond their work environments.

Drawing from our two outstanding examples in addition to my own consulting experiences, I have identified a few rules of thumb that can serve as guidelines for any company wishing to sustain an atmosphere of fun in its corporate environment. The rules serve as barometers of the corporate culture, in that, if they cannot be adhered to, it is likely that, as with the company in Example I, fear will in time overtake fun as the prevailing energy, despite the best of intentions. Wherever possible, I will try to cite illustrative real-life examples of the rules in action.

1. The Rule of No Fear

The reason fun-based initiatives often turn in time to fear-based, is that insufficient attention was paid to eliminating fear right at the beginning. If humor beings are at their best when they are having fun, then the most successful companies will have a playground environment that is as free of fear as possible. W. Edwards Deming, the father of Total Quality Management, wrote in his landmark book, *Out of Crisis* (Cambridge: MIT Press, 1982), "Drive out fear throughout the organization, so that everybody may work effectively and more productively for the company."

In 1992, Georg Bauer became president of Mercedes-Benz Credit Corporation, whose five hundred employees executed a portfolio of $9 billion in vehicle loans. On the surface the corporation was doing fine, but Mr. Bauer foresaw the need to reorganize it, cutting costs and improving customer services, in order to be prepared for future trends in the marketplace.

Announcing his intention to change things "from the bottom up," he decided to charge the employees with the responsibility of finding the weaknesses in the organization. Every job and every procedure was fair game for change. He knew that to affect this initiative he would have to inspire the deepest most creative responses of everyone in the organization. So, he instituted one immutable rule—no fear.

Bauer knew that only by breaking down fears and turf guarding, and encouraging experimentation, risk-taking and, even, play, could he hope to accomplish the restructuring. He encouraged leaders to support people who were willing to take risks and make mistakes. He insisted upon a fearless environment.

The no-fear rule was accompanied by a promise from Bauer. Despite his eagerness to cut costs, he guaranteed that no one would be laid off, no matter how many new efficiencies were introduced. He truly created a "safe sandbox" for people to play in.
(Thomas Petzinger, *The New Pioneers*, Simon & Schuster, 1999)

Southwest Airline's corporate position on encouraging employees to take risks is very straightforward:
"The costs of getting burned once in a while are insignificant compared to the benefits that come from people feeling free to take risks and be creative."
(Freiberg and Freiberg, *Nuts!*; Bard Press, 1996)

2. The Rule of Shared Power
This rule covers a lot of cultural ground. It starts with listening carefully to your personnel. Outside consultants may be helpful, but the effective answers to a company's problems will usually come from within. In retrospect, another mistake that the company in Example I probably made was to listen exclusively to its consultants and not to its employees. By the time its new initiatives were announced, they came across as answers imposed on the work force, rather than questions asked of them.

But, it goes beyond listening at the beginning. Continuous listening is required to sustain the Fun Factor. Tom's of Maine, Inc., a successful manufacturer of personal care products, understands this need. Here is President and co-founder Tom Chappell's description of his approach:

"We do something at Tom's of Maine that I think is unique; we have a curriculum for teaching our mission within the company. Once every three months the whole company gets together for this purpose. We spend the morning together focusing on one aspect: profitability, diversity, the environment – values we've held up in our mission. It costs us about $75,000 each time in lost production, and it's worth every penny.

"Our managers and staff come away from those experiences with recommendations, which then are gathered and taken to the appropriate department heads. So we take the fruits of every intentional learning environment and transfer them into a very practical environment. Doing this helps improve everyone's consciousness about having our practicalities reflect our values. It's a morale booster for everyone and helps build fellowship and team skills. It shows the company is serious about walking its talk.

"… The analysts wonder what effect this has on our bottom line. When we need to call upon the reserves of our people – to dig in deeper, meet extraordinary goals—we can expect it here. It's a give-and-take relationship such that we're giving to our people the benefits, tangible and intangible, and they're giving us their highest performance, their greatest ideas on how to solve problems."

—Tom Chappell, cofounder and CEO, Tom's of Maine
(Cohen and Greenfield, *Ben & Jerry's Double-Dip*: Fireside, 1997)

Sharing the power can even go beyond continuous listening, when it's done right. The following account is excerpted from a fascinating book, *The New Pioneers*, written by Thomas Petzinger, Jr. (Simon & Schuster, 1999). It involves a manufacturing company, Monarch Marketing, that reinvented itself from within:

"In 1995, Monarch Marketing came under new ownership by private investors, who installed a turnaround artist named John Paxton as chief executive. Paxton was appalled when touring the plant for the first time—the workers blankly repeating the same motions, machinery bolted in the same location for decades. The manufacturing operation, he recognized, would be a ball and chain on whatever efforts the company launched to reinvigorate the product line and sales effort. 'Without the shop floor behind us, we'd have limited success in everything else we did,' he explained.

"Paxton brought in a hard-charging, gravel-voiced production chief named Jerry Schlaegel, who, in turn, recruited a hyperkinetic quality-assurance engineer he knew named Steve Schneider. Their outward manners might have easily led one to mistake them for classic Industrial Age managers, Schlaegel with his gruffness, Schneider with his zealotry. But after spending several years on high-tech shop floors they had acquired a keen respect for the mind of the worker and for the combined mind of workers— and for the difficulty of unlocking them. Every program to put this knowledge into action seemed to fail miserably, not just at Monarch, but just about every plant they knew of.

"Schneider and Schlaegel brooded at length over these failures. In time they realized that most companies treated worker-involvement programs as corporate cure-alls, as turnarounds in a pill. Promising the moon, consultants designed these programs so broadly they could accomplish nothing specific. Instead of attacking down-to-earth problems like parts flow or cycle time, these programs invariably wound up in amorphous issues ("worker morale") or trifling ones (more picnic tables for outdoor lunch breaks). Just as vexing, meetings invariably led to more meetings.

"Schneider and Schlaegel decided to involve the shop floor in ways that avoided problems, combining intellectual freedom with the kind of discipline demanded of a commercial enterprise. Although it had not occurred to them in precisely these terms, they needed "a small set of simple rules."

Their first rule was an uncustomary one: Participation in the new exchange of knowledge would be compulsory, not voluntary. That simple rule altered the entire cast of the initiative. This was not a sop to employees, not a feel-good thing, not "empowerment." Indeed it was ridiculous to think that employees needed "power." They already had power! The power was in their heads! Schneider told people that Monarch was paying them to work and from that point forward they would be expected to bring along their brains. Every employee in the shop would receive training in problem solving and team communications, and anyone, at one time or another, might be required to sit on a team studying ways to improve the processes of the shop floor.

But how could they ground the process in meaningful business issues, in things that could be changed rather than merely talked about? Schneider and Schlaegel realized that every genuine problem in manufacturing can be measured. All told, Schneider identified 162 measurable variables—"metrics," he called them – involving everything from traditional quality and productivity statistics to such unusual indices as the number of unsolicited letters of commendation received from customers. Teams would form only with the intention of improving one or more specific metrics. There would be no open-ended, pie-in-the-sky committees.

There were just a few more rules. Teams not only had to come up with their own solution to a problem, they had to implement it as well. If other departments had to make changes, it was the team's duty to persuade them to do so. If vendors had to change how they served the factory, the team was charged with making the necessary arrangements. Combining ideas and implementation would motivate people to think hard for the most practical possible solution. 'This is your job! This is your life!' Schneider told people. 'Change it! Just go make it happen and tell us about it when you're through. In fact, you are required to make the changes and tell us when you're done.'

The final rule: No project would last longer than thirty days, from the formation of the team to the implementation of the solution. 'It's a project,' Schneider told people, 'not a process.'

"Those were the only rules. Anyone could create a team, management or labor. Anything and everything in the plant was fair game for review—so long as it could be measured. A team could come up with any solution at all—so long as it was willing to carry it out on the shop floor. Management foreswore any and all veto rights. There were no limits on spending. Schneider and Schlaegel drew a deep breath, gulped, and rolled out the new rules.

"… By the time it was all over they had reduced the square footage of the assembly area by 70 percent, freeing up space for new products. They had cut their work-in-progress inventory by $127,000. They had slashed past-due shipments by 90 percent. Best of all, they had doubled their productivity.

"… Before long Monarch's operating income hit an all-time high. The company's adroit application of knowledge received many commendations. Schneider and Schlaegel began freely teaching "practical process improvement,' as they called it, to Monarch's suppliers and customers. Most interesting of all, a new culture emerged spontaneously within the workforce—a culture that did not permit but that insisted on brain work. Even those who were the most cynical to begin with became eager converts."

This kind of power sharing seems courageous only to those who cannot trust the nature of the humor beings with whom they work. To those who know the potential of the Fun Factor, it is no more risky than any other sound business investment. "I've never had control and I never wanted it," writes Herb Kelleher of Southwest Airlines. "If you create an environment where people truly participate, you don't need control. They know what needs to be done and they do it." (*Leader to Leader*, Spring, 1997)

Sustaining an atmosphere of fun requires leaders who are willing to be led at times by the wisdom of their "followers." If you would like more encouragement and inspiration regarding this kind of mutuality, I recommend the book, *Out of Control: The New Biology of Machines, Social Systems, and the Economic World*, by Kevin Kelly (Addison-Wesley, 1994).

3. The Rule of No Intramural Rivalries

This rule addresses the fine line between competition and rivalry within an organization. When we discussed rewarding and reinforcing the Fun Factor in the family (Chapter 4), we recognized competition as a valuable element, noting that it can make a process more interesting and engaging, and that it can serve as a stimulus to excellent performance. The same can be said of competition in the corporate environment.

Yet, if competition goes too far, just as it sets up sibling rivalries in the family, it can lead to intramural rivalries in a company. This produces tension, fears of favoritism, and ultimately stratification into "winners and losers." When this occurs, the fear factor takes over, usually signaled by resentments and jealousies, which undermine any team effort.

As with the fun-filled family, the best way to avoid the deterioration of competition into rivalry is to introduce all competition in the spirit of fun, by focusing more upon effort than upon outcome. In this regard, the difference between incentives and rewards can be critical. Incentives communicate a "carrot-on-the-stick' image, suggesting that the "prize" is the reason for the effort. This is a rather cynical appraisal of what motivates one's personnel. At best we might call it uninspiring.

Rewards communicate a different message. They express the expectation that effort comes from the joy of doing one's best, and, in that sense, is its own reward. The rewards or awards offered by the company are reflections or acknowledgments of recognized effort, not the stimuli for it. At Cheap Joe's Art Stuff in Boone, North Carolina, employees receive "Smiley Face" cards for above and beyond work, redeemable for $15 prize certificates, as well as "You Done Good" ribbons for positive customer feedback. The message here is inspiring to employees for at least two reasons: (a) it calls for a higher level of commitment, and (b) it confirms that positive effort is being observed and appreciated.

The critical difference becomes even more apparent when we watch how these two scenarios play out. As with the unfortunate company in Example I, the incentive scenario inevitably creates a preoccupation with the relative scarcity of prizes. Unless the bar is set so low as to be virtually meaningless, over time there are bound to be more losers than winners. This is precisely what happened. As soon as all of the most obvious "waste" had been identified, the individual efforts to continue finding inefficiencies went unrecognized. Only the results counted.

However, when the emphasis is on recognizing and appreciating effort, there is no scarcity of opportunity. There is no limit on winners. If you and I are both making laudable efforts in the workplace, we can both be rewarded, and your reward takes nothing away from mine. In fact, our rewards, far from discouraging our colleagues, will only serve to inspire them to put forth similar efforts. Everyone wins.

The bottom line is that an incentive program is an admission that there is a scarcity of recognition available in the organization, as well as an invitation for the employees to fight over the relatively few "crumbs" on the table. In contrast, a rewards program celebrates the potential of every employee to make a laudable effort and invites each to step up to be recognized and appreciated.

An example of the a rewards program that works is Southwest Airline's Winning Spirit Awards:

"Every other month, the company honors ten to twelve employees whose actions make them living examples of Southwest's values and philosophy. The Winning Spirit Awards are given to employees nominated by other employees (or sometimes by customers) across Southwest's system. Sunny Divjak, manager of cultural activities, heads the committee of nine that makes the selections. Each recipient is invited to a presentation held in the executive boardroom at Southwest's headquarters building. Herb (Kelleher) reads the letter of nomination sent in for each recipient and gives each a Winning Spirit lapel pin and two positive-space passes on Southwest Airlines. Each honoree gets a framed photo taken with Herb as a follow-up gift, and a group photograph is published in LUV Lines, along with an inspirational quote and a summary of each person's 'winning spirit'."
(Freiberg and Freiberg, *Nuts!*, Bard Press, 1996)

"I have no idea how many different awards and recognition ceremonies we have, but it has shown us all that this company is big on 'thank yous'."

—John Farry, flight attendant, Southwest Airlines

4. The Rule of Constant Renewal

An environment of fun, no matter how painstakingly constructed, cannot be sustained without a careful plan to carry it forward in perpetuity. In order to permanently affect the company culture, the Fun Factor must outlive those responsible for its creation. Therefore, plans for constant renewal must be identified and put into action from day one.

For a great example of this, we once again turn to Southwest Airlines:

"Southwest instituted a mechanism in 1990 for the sole purpose of perpetuating the Southwest Spirit. The Culture Committee (one of only a very few standing committees) has become an inspired team of more than a hundred storytellers who are the company's ambassadors and missionaries. 'We're not big on committees at Southwest,' (CEO) Kelleher states, 'but of the committees we do have, the Culture Committee is the most important!'

"Southwest's Culture Committee is an example of people working together to create covenantal relationships. Committee members are zealots when it comes to the continuation of Southwest's family feel. The committee represents everyone from flight attendants and reservationists to top executives. It is not a group of headquarters staff and managers who use their power to tell the rest of the organization how to think and behave. Rather it is a group of shamans, spiritual teachers, and organizational storytellers … The committee works behind the scenes to foster Southwest's commitment to values such as profitability, low cost, family, love, and fun."

(Freiberg and Freiberg, *Nuts!*, Bard Press, 1996)

Southwest is by no means the only company that has succeeded in "institutionalizing" its fun. Eastman Kodak has its Humor Task Force, Sun Microsystems its annual April Fool's Day ritual, Ben & Jerry's its "Joy Gang", and Digital Equipment its "Grouch Patrol" and humor support groups, just to name a few. Cheap Joe's Art Stuff charges an Employee Activity Committee

(AEC) with the responsibility of planning special staff events, such as Easter Egg Hunts, Valentine's Day Breakfasts and "Volleyball Fever." What each of these companies has in common is the effort to incorporate the Fun Factor in such a fashion as to make it impossible to ignore as times change and the organization matures. The common thread of all successful efforts is constant celebration.

As predicted, we come back once again to the act of celebrating. Reinforcing the Fun Factor is all about habitual celebration. And the most successful celebrations for any company are those that focus on people rather than products. Nowhere is the model of the fun-filled family more applicable in the business environment.

Celebration is what fearless families do best, whether it is for a birth, a graduation, a wedding, or a cherished holiday. The more closely your company can resemble a functional family capitalizing on every opportunity to create celebration rituals, the more likely will be its chances of sustaining and reinforcing an atmosphere for fun.

Chapter Eight

THE CARE AND FEEDING OF YOUR HUMOR NATURE

Now that we have explored how the Fun Factor operates in family life and in the workplace, it is time to look within ourselves to more fully understand the marvelous and miraculous personal resource that makes fun possible. The truth of the matter is that this amazing force we call fun does not originate in the external structures and rituals of family or work. Neither is it rooted in the many effective strategies we have described. This healing, uplifting, excellence-promoting energy comes from one source only—people —you, me, and every other individual member of family or workplace groups.

Therefore, if we are to reap the benefits of more fun-filled, fearless homes and businesses, it falls to each individual to do his or her part. The best strategies and the most creative rituals will not be enough, unless you and I each bring to the table a vibrant and well cared-for sense of humor or humor nature, as I prefer to call it.

The care and maintenance of your humor nature is a responsibility that only you can undertake. Others can support you and help create a healthy fun-filled environment but, in the end, you must do what is necessary to keep your humor nature strong and effective. This chapter is dedicated to helping you do just that.

What is Humor Nature?

Why do I refer to your sense of humor as your humor nature? The answer is both simple and profound. To me, humor is much more than a coping tool. I think it is the essence of any human being.

Therefore, I believe humor nature is the pure truth about you and me. It is the deepest, widest and highest part of us. It is the source of every characteristic we value in one another – integrity, hope, resilience, optimism, creativity, tenacity, generosity, mischievousness, forgiveness, community and love. At our best, we accurately reflect our humor nature. It needs no elaboration or embellishment. That's why I have suggested that the term humor being is synonymous with human being.

Just as human nature is the tangible evidence of human spirit, so is humor nature a measure of your humor spirit. Humor spirit is the breath that gives us life. It is our perfection, unadulterated by our perfectionism. Fun is nothing less than the energy of the humor spirit. No wonder it is indomitable when it is released without restraint. It is the strongest force in the world.

Yet, in one of life's strangest paradoxes, humor nature can at times be remarkably fragile. Since it speaks in a whisper, it can often be overridden by louder voices. Since it is childlike in its simplicity, it can sometimes be shamed and intimidated by the harsh judgment of more powerful adult pretensions. Since it always reflects the truth it can be unwelcome whenever we would rather harbor a fantasy or self-delusion.

Without care and maintenance, your humor nature will languish in the recesses of your awareness, virtually useless for anything more than occasional entertainment. You might even become afraid of it and choose to deliberately repress it. This would truly be a tragic instance of becoming your own worst enemy. Therefore, I want to recommend some ways to prevent this from happening.

What follows are nine suggestions for strengthening and maintaining your humor nature. They are not strategies. They are mental disciplines that will become habits of thought, as you allow yourself to pursue them. Each will strengthen your trust in your humor nature and in time will help you give it more prominence in your day-to-day awareness.

1. <u>Always ask the basic maintenance question—Am I having fun?</u>
At this point, I hope you are persuaded that the question, "Am I having fun?" is neither frivolous nor irresponsible. I believe it is the most serious and responsible question you can ever ask, because, short of having fun, you can never be at your best. That's just the way it is for any humor being.

Keeping in mind that fun is nothing more than the energy of your humor nature, you will realize that, by asking, "Am I having fun?" you are simply taking a reading of your energy level. If your answer is "No," then, just like when your car is low on gasoline, it's time to stop and refuel. How often would we run out of gas if we ignored the gauges on our dashboard? The same diligence should be applied to our personal "fuel reserves."

I think when we fail to assess our awareness of fun, we run the risk of running on empty, or, as often happens without notice, switching to our alternative fuel – fear. There is always plenty of that available. Other people will give it to you free of charge. However, you know by now that fear is not a reliable fuel for the long haul. "Refueling" with fun is a much better idea.

Whenever you take the measure of your humor nature, do not be misled or distracted by the misinformation you have previously acquired about fun. You are not asking, "Am I laughing?" Nor are you inquiring, "Am I being funny?" As you now know, fun has almost nothing to do with laughter and jokes; it has to do with joy.

To fully express your humor nature you must have the intention to enjoy whatever you are doing. If you get to do what you enjoy, that's great. Just be forewarned. It won't last. If you are not lucky enough to be doing what you enjoy, then I challenge you to either change what you are doing, or, if that's not possible, strive to enjoy whatever you must do. It's a matter of intention.

Grady, a physician specializing in internal medicine, was

diagnosed with insulin-dependent diabetes at age 45. Eighteen months later he described his progress in adjusting to the demands of his disease:

"At first I was furious at God and myself, and jealous of everybody else," he said. "It didn't seem fair that, after working so hard to earn the means to enjoy myself, I had to limit my lifestyle so dramatically. Then I began to listen to my patients, many of whom have more severe restrictions than I. Who was I to complain?"

He continued. "So, I decided I could choose either to be resentful, angry and reluctant about my fate, or grateful that I had a game plan and a way to monitor my success in following it. As soon as I chose the second alternative, I noticed I had more energy and enthusiasm for everything."

"Don't get me wrong," he added. "I still would rather not have diabetes. It's just a little easier since I switched my attitude."

What is fun for you? It could be anything from watching a beautiful sunset to hearing a good joke, and many things in between. Personal enjoyment is a very subjective thing. The specifics may be different from one person to the next, but, generally speaking, fun usually involves feeling good about oneself. It is difficult to enjoy anything, if you don't feel as though you deserve to. Consequently, to ask the question, "Am I having fun?" requires self-esteem.

In a similar vein, when we become aware of not having fun, we will have trouble fixing the situation, if we do not deem ourselves worthy of the effort. Many of us suffer from a lifelong exposure to the so-called "puritan ethic," which teaches that anything that feels good is categorically wrong. For some, a sense of unworthiness involves a deeper and more serious problem that may require professional help. In any case, it is well worth the effort to remove obstacles that stand in the way of exercising our intention to have fun, no matter what the circumstance.

2. Be pro-active in scheduling fun activities for yourself.
Taking good care of your humor nature requires a degree of selfishness. This may at first make you uncomfortable. After all, weren't we all raised to consider the needs of others first? That's a

wonderful sentiment, but I have one small problem with it. It's not good for your health, emotionally, physically, economically, socially, or any other way. Health at any level requires that you place your needs at the highest priority. Your humor nature recognizes this truth and will always be for you first. Your responsibility is to go along with it.

Please don't misunderstand me. I am talking about your needs, not your wants. I am advocating selfishness, not self-centeredness. Even on your best day, I don't think you represent the center of the universe. Nonetheless, I believe your health and well being ought to be at the top of your list of things to be maintained. And that is the whole point of this mental habit. Your fun should not have to wait until you have the more "responsible" obligations out of the way. Being pro-active about fun means scheduling it first.

There's only one way to do this. Select something to do purely for the fun of it. It can be going to the movies, taking a walk, or taking a nap, but make sure it is something you will enjoy. Then make a date with yourself and keep it. You wouldn't think of standing up somebody you liked, so don't do it to yourself. Honor the obligation you've made to your humor nature.

I used to think that Garfield the Cat's quote, "Life is short! Eat dessert first!" was a joke, until I met my friend, Alma.

Alma is a 72-year-old woman who, since her husband died of cancer fifteen years ago, has been volunteering daily as a receptionist at a local cancer center. Everyone who passes through the doors of that center finds Alma's energy and enthusiasm remarkable. Despite all the fearful and sad things she witnesses, as people struggle desperately to survive their cancers, she never seems to have a bad day. Her good cheer and optimism are constantly at a high level.

One day I commended her on her seemingly boundless supply of good will and positive thoughts, and I asked her how she did it.

She winked at me and said, "I schedule my vacations first."

"How does that help?" I wondered.

"Probably not the way you think," she responded. "I love to travel. So, that's the first thing I plan every year. And I tell the clinic manager every January which weeks I'll be gone for the whole year. She knows that, no matter what else is going on in the clinic for those weeks, my time off is not negotiable."

"So, by looking forward to your upcoming trips, you can maintain your rosy disposition through thick and thin," I commented.

"Not exactly," she cautioned me. "My trips aren't my compensation for working in this environment. The work I do doesn't make me need a reward. It's the other way around. The trips make me want to do this work. I come here to give back the joy I get from traveling."

I wonder if that's what Garfield has been trying to tell us all along.

Alma's distinction is a subtle but critical one. It underlines the concept of pro-activity and it will enable you to unleash the full power of this mental habit. If you schedule fun activities to reward or compensate yourself for hard work, or to provide an incentive for working harder, you will be missing the point. Fun is the fuel that makes the hard work possible and, as such, we are wise to fill our tanks in advance.

3. Reject the #1 fun-killer—guilt

This may sound like a strange sentiment coming from a psychiatrist, but I think the concept of guilt is, for the most part, bogus. If you were to tell me you were guilty, I would take it to mean that you had deliberately or accidentally done something wrong, and were now recognizing the error of your ways. That would make sense. My advice to you would be to make restitution, as best you could, and, while paying your debt, try to learn from your mistake. Then leave your mistake where it belongs—in the past—and concentrate on present realities.

If you were to tell me you were feeling guilt, I would take it to mean that you were attempting to prop up your over-sized ego by taking responsibility for something you had no control over, and thus, by your suffering, prove that you really have that much power, should you ever choose to use it. That would make no sense at all. In which case, my advice would be, "Get over it!"

Guilty is a verdict. Guilt is an ego trip. It enables you to remain self-centered, while appearing to be focused on others. Your humor nature respects a verdict, but will have no truck with an inflated ego. It recognizes guilt as a fear-based manipulation, inspired by an egotistical refusal to accept realistic limitations. If you want to support your humor nature you must let go of guilt.

One of my mentors at the University of Louisville was Wayne E. Oates, regarded by many as the "dean of hospital chaplains" in America. Wayne was a professor in our department of psychiatry, where he directed his nationally renowned training program in ethics and pastoral counseling. He was also a dear friend.

One day, I heard him say something in a lecture that contradicted what he had written in one of his many successful books. When I brought it to his attention, he began laughing.

"I'm laughing at myself," he explained. "I can remember a time when it would upset me to have my inconsistencies pointed out. I would feel guilty and go to great lengths to rationalize the contradictions. At some point, I realized it was never going to stop and I didn't want to spend all that energy feeling guilty. So, I decided I could always be of some use, even if I'm imperfect. Even on my worst day, I can still serve as a bad example."

Feeling guilty is a choice. It comes from second-guessing things that are already history. It cannot be forced upon us. But, sometimes we welcome it because it makes us seem like noble, responsible people. For one thing, you are noble already. You needn't do anything to prove it. For another, wallowing in guilt is a most irresponsible preoccupation.

When we choose guilt, we choose to remain with the past, instead of focusing on the present. What a clever way to avoid being responsible, as we appear to be suffering under the burden of heavy accountability, supported by delusions of power that would have embarrassed Napoleon Bonaparte. By focusing on the past, guilt also effectively prevents fun, because fun, as you know, resides only in the present moment.

I sometimes choose to feel guilty in hopes that it will encourage others to go easy on me. ("Don't punish him; he already feels guilty.") It never works. In fact, it usually backfires. I apparently present myself as so unworthy that those around me hardly think twice about treating me that way. Pretty soon I start believing I deserve their contempt.

Playing host to guilt puts us at increased risk for depression. I am not saying that depressed persons cause their depressions. I don't really know what causes depression. I'm simply suggesting that, in the same way that exposure to a chill might lower our resistance to a cold, depression becomes more likely when we linger over guilt.

The antidote to guilt is to get over it. Forgive yourself for being imperfect and do something good for somebody right now. But don't do it as penance for past mistakes. Do it as a celebration that, even on your worst day, you have a lot of good in you that can be shared.

4. Use the humor relaxations—breathing.
I rushed into the group therapy room flushed with excitement. "Sorry I'm late," I blurted. "I just finished the most exciting phone call."

"Well, don't make us beg!" said Tony. "What's the good news?"

Every member of the group knew by my expression that something exciting had happened for my speaking career. Having been a part of the creation of the Laugh Doctor from the beginning, they took a proprietary interest in every step of his growing popularity. They were eager to hear about their latest opportunity to "share" me with the outside world.

"A big east coast agency just called," I told them. "They have a last minute opening in a program they are preparing. They offered me eight minutes to do my thing in front of an audience of very influential people. If I do well, it could open a lot of doors for the Laugh Doctor. The only catch is that the program is next Tuesday, less than a week away."

The group responded with a chorus of congratulations and reassurances:

"No problem! You're going to blow them away."

"Aren't you going to take us with you?"

"Please don't forget us when you become famous."

There was a momentary silence.

Then Darlene whispered, "Don't forget to breathe."

It probably goes without saying, but let me remind you just in case. Remembering to breathe is critical to almost everything in life, including the care and maintenance of a healthy humor nature. Darlene's advice was wise on many levels. Inhaling and exhaling are fundamental processes that are firmly grounded in the present moment. By placing our respirations on "automatic pilot," we give ourselves license to look ahead into the future or linger over the past. But all it takes is a brief interruption of our breath to refocus us with alarming speed and accuracy to the here and now.

Therefore, whenever we are willing to pay more attention to our breathing, the chances are we will incorporate more of the present moment and release more of our distractions. We inhale the now and exhale everything else. This is beneficial to your humor nature because, like your breath, it is firmly rooted in the moment. When you increase your awareness of your breath, you also increase your awareness of your humor nature.

You needn't be a world-class meditator to derive the benefits of conscious breathing. Simple breathing exercises are an excellent way to do this. In chapter one we introduced you to one or two. Here is one more that will teach you a lot about your humor nature while giving it a chance to show you its stuff.

Sit calmly in a comfortable chair in a quiet room.

Close your eyes and take in a deep breath.

Without holding the breath, release it at about the same pace as you took it in.

Take in another breath, and, as you do, loosen your belly, so your chest can expand fully.

Again, do not hold the breath, but, like water would flow

over a dam, release it spontaneously and effortlessly as soon as your chest is full.

Find an easy, comfortable rhythm of breathing in and out and, as you adopt that rhythm for your breath, begin saying to yourself the words, "I am" with each breath in, "relaxed" with each breath out. Repeat these words with each breath in and out for about a dozen breaths, letting go of all your tension every time you say the word "relaxed."

After a dozen or so breaths, discontinue the words "I am—relaxed," but continue the rhythm of breathing that you have established.

In this relaxed state, as you continue your easy rhythmic breathing, turn your attention to something that is amusing to you. It can be anything—a joke you heard, a movie you saw, or a funny thing that happened to you—anything that would bring a smile to your face. It doesn't have to be something funny. Perhaps you will want to think of a beautiful scene or a baby's smile—just so it makes you want to smile.

Give this amusing image or memory your full and undivided attention and as you "play" it over and over in your mind's eye, allow yourself to enjoy it each time, smiling and even laughing if you feel like it.

After enjoying your amusing image or memory several times, let it go, and bring your focus back to your regular rhythm of breathing and to the accompanying phrase, "I am – relaxed." Repeat the phrase with another dozen breaths.

Then end the exercise by taking a long, deep breath in, slowly releasing that breath, as you slowly open your eyes and stretch your arms over your head.

5. Smiling

Smiling is without a doubt the single most effective and efficient thing we can do to maintain the vitality of our humor natures. As we've already observed, smiling offers remarkable benefits physically, psychologically and socially. A smile is silent, unobtrusive and totally portable. You can take a smile anywhere, and well you should, because it is sometimes hard to find one when you need it.

The muscles involved in smiling must be hard-wired to the energy centers in your brain, because every time you put one on your face, you can depend on feeling a surge of energy and confidence. At the same time, the sight of your smile has a profound effect on the rest of us. We want to be closer to you. We want to hear what you have to say. We can't resist your magnetic drawing power. This is all welcome news for your humor nature.

It was Improv Night at our local comedy club. As a part-time member of one of the groups, I was invited to join them for their performance. The evening was going well. We were having fun and so was the audience (it usually works that way).

For one of the games, the troupe offered to act out a scene designed completely by the audience. In addition to time, place and situation, the audience also assigned characters and characteristics to all the players. My character was designated as "Mister Happy" and my assignment was to say no words and to smile constantly throughout.

As the scene unfolded, I began to notice something interesting. Every time someone looked at my ever-smiling face, he or she couldn't help laughing. I wasn't saying anything, nor was I very prominent in the action. But the audience found the big constant grin irresistibly funny and they kept coming back for more. I was a big hit by just keeping my mouth shut and smiling.

But that was only half of it. While the "eternal" smile was captivating the audience it was having a second effect on me. I noticed that my performance was flowing more freely. I was more tuned in to my fellow players and more spontaneous with my actions and reactions. I felt more confidence in my ideas. Smiling made me a more valuable contributor to the group effort, and a more successful performer.

The next time you attend a comedy performance, notice how often the comedian smiles. I'll bet it will be frequently, if not continuously. It won't be because he's laughing at his own jokes.

Nor will it be a defensive maneuver. Chances are he'll be smiling because he's learned that the audience has more fun and he gives a better performance if he remembers to smile. He's discovered that his humor nature is stronger when he's smiling.

Even though you are not trying to give a comedy performance, you will have the same experience. Your smile will strengthen your humor nature every time. Think of it as a refueling mechanism. Whenever you're smiling, you're filling your tank. Since your smile is completely portable, you can be like those planes that refuel in mid-air.

Here's a tip. A great time to refuel is while you are sleeping. So, try this. Take something to bed with you that will make you smile as you fall off to sleep. My wife claims she's very lucky in this respect. For the last 38 years she's gotten to go to bed with me. I choose to take that as a compliment, so let's drop it right there.

Since most of you are not as lucky as she, you might want to watch a funny video, read an amusing story, or just think only pleasant thoughts as you drift off to sleep. If you doze off while smiling, you may smile more in your sleep and wake up with the smile still on your face. What a great way to start the day.

6. Imaging good outcomes

What the mind perceives, the body believes. Did you know that most of what you see and hear is a reflection of what you think? We are not objective observers of anything. Even science, long the epitome of detached objectivity, has discovered that a "passive" observer is not outside the equation, but interacts with the other components in ways that influence the outcome.

Since we have no hope of being entirely neutral, our only choice is to decide what impact we are going to have in any situation. Toward which outcome do we want to lend our influence? As co-creators of the results, what do we want to see?

Imagination is the strongest element in our creative arsenal. Have you ever wondered why imagination contains the word image? I believe it is because we create visually. That is we see things in our mind long before we see them with our eyes. Put another way, when

156

you see something first in your mind's eyes, you are more likely to see it with your physical eyes. What your mind perceives, your body believes.

Athletes have learned to capitalize on the "predictive" power of imagining or imaging. For example, if a basketball player wants to improve her free throw shooting accuracy, she can stand at the free throw line and shoot 100 free throws every day; or she can once a day close her eyes and image herself shooting 100 free throws accurately. It has been proven that either of those choices will result in measurable improvement in her accuracy.

What works for an athlete will work for any of us. Imaging will have a powerful influence on the results we get from our efforts. Since the visual is the strongest and most universal component of humor, it figures that imagination plays a major role in humor nature. Therefore, by imaging the outcomes of your behavior, you are inviting your humor nature to be stronger and more active. What the mind perceives, the body believes.

The best way to capitalize on the power of visualization is to start small and build up gradually, as you prove to yourself it works. I recommend the following exercise as an initial daily routine. It takes less than a minute.

Sit quietly with your eyes closed and concentrate on something small that is on your agenda in the next hour or two. It shouldn't be the most challenging thing. In fact, at first it might be better to choose something more mundane, something you might otherwise take for granted. For example you might choose reading the paper, eating a sandwich, or changing a light bulb. Come to think of it, there have been days when those are my most challenging tasks. The important point here is it must be something you are sure to do within the next couple of hours.

With your eyes still closed, visualize yourself doing the simple behavior, as though you were watching yourself on a TV monitor (Smile, you're on candid camera!). Since you are the creator and director of this brief visualization, make sure that you see yourself derive supreme satisfaction from completing the task. Watch yourself getting the most enjoyment ever from reading the paper, or savoring the delicious flavor of your peanut butter and jelly sandwich, or changing the bulb without burning your fingers, whatever represents maximum enjoyment for you.

That's it. You're done. Now get up and go about doing whatever you've planned. When you get to the "task" you visualized, you will notice two things. You will have more fun doing it and you will be more aware of how much fun you're having. That's because, by "previewing" your behavior, you invited your humor nature to be more involved when you got around to doing it. We already know that having more fun leads to greater success. If it works with jelly sandwiches, think of the possibilities when you apply it to bigger projects.

7. Houseclean your small irritations and pet peeves

Irritations and pet peeves get in the way of your humor nature's full and free expression. It's like trying to write on a cluttered desk. It's cramped and confining. I know about cluttered desks. I've heard and used all of the rationalizations for not keeping mine cleared off, including the one designed to back down anyone who is kind enough to offer to clean it up for me— "I know where everything is. Don't touch a thing!"

Speaking as a world-class desk clutterer, I can tell you exactly how it happens. Paper and books don't usually arrive in piles. They accumulate over days, weeks, and months, one piece at a time, until one day the entire surface is buried and I've forgotten where the phone is.

I recall a Beetle Bailey cartoon strip that depicted Beetle reading all the memos tacked to a jam-packed army bulletin board. The deeper he dug into the layers of paper, the further back went the dates of the messages, until he found the last one. It was a notice for everyone to meet at Valley Forge, signed by George Washington.

It's the same with humor beings as with desktops and bulletin boards. It's not the big things that bury us. It's the minor irritations, setbacks and disappointments that accumulate below our radar screens, until one day, we can't see our way out. The responsibility for this happening, both on our desks and in our lives, can be placed squarely on our own shoulders.

The accumulation is caused by a lack of discipline on our part, a failure to respond in a timely fashion. Things pile up because we hesitate to decide and dispense with them. It's a subtle form of procrastination, for which we pay a high price.

Much of this has to do with our difficulty in letting go. For some it's the fear of losing control; for others it might be the risk of making the wrong decision. Regardless of the dynamics, when we fail to release things, we are up against a natural law. The longer we hold onto something, the harder it becomes to let go.

The antidote is very simple, though not always easy. Do not postpone your responses. Say this slowly to yourself: "There is no such thing as once and for all." Deal immediately with each issue that lands on your emotional desk in the best way you can. Once you've done that, let it go. If you make a bad choice, as you sometimes will, you'll probably get another shot at it. But don't linger over the issue or second-guess yourself. Let it seek you out again.

Remember, we are not talking about the major catastrophes of your life. We all recognize there are many situations that require something more of us than a quick response. This is all the more reason to deal with the minor irritations in a timely fashion. If you keep current with the smaller things, the big things won't be as overwhelming.

By postponing your responses, you not only invite the cluttered desk syndrome, but you also disable your humor nature. When you refuse to let go of pet peeves, you are effectively putting off your fun. Fun cannot be postponed. If you don't have fun now, it won't be any easier to have fun later.

Your humor nature stands ready to help you immediately, if you are willing to clear off your desk.

8. Look for the positive in everything

Once again, we come around to one of our most effective strategies for fun—Always Look for the Pony. It should not surprise us that a mental habit reflecting this strategy will prove beneficial to your humor nature.

You may balk at the suggestion to look for the positive in everything, because you don't want to be naïve. Is it naïve to know that the race is not always to the swift? Is it naïve to recognize that sometimes the worst tragedies evolve into strong blessings? Is it naïve to believe that the meek will ultimately inherit the earth? I'd say there is plenty of wisdom, drawn from real life experiences, to support this kind of naiveté. Why not be an optimist?

Or perhaps you're afraid of being disappointed, if you allow your hopes to get too high. Since you're not perfect, you're bound to be disappointed sometimes. Let me share what Jerry Lewis has to say about this kind of risk.

"Here's what I think about risk," says Jerry Lewis, with just a touch of impatience in his voice. "There's risk in everything. There's risk in crossing the street, eating in a restaurant or driving your car. There's even risk in getting out of bed each morning, or staying in bed, for that matter. You just can't avoid risk, if you're alive."

"I've always believed," he continues, "that if you lined ten people against a wall and offered to hug each one, seven would hug you back and three would turn you down. On a good day, you'd get eight; on a great day, nine. You never get ten."

"Now, here's what you have to ask yourself," he concludes. "Are you going to pass up seven hugs because of the risk of three rejections? I'll take those odds anytime. That's why I'm an optimist about the human condition."

I want to remind you that this is not a philosophical debate. It doesn't matter how full or empty the proverbial glass is. A decision to always look for the positive can be based on the reality that there's always a pony in every pile of manure. It is not easy but, if we are willing to persist in that expectation, we will find the positive elements in anything.

Helen, a 37-year-old woman recovering from breast cancer, reported the following exchange she had with her oncologist during her chemotherapy.

"My hair had begun falling out in large clumps," she said,

"and Dr. Franklin seemed more upset about it than I was. He was telling me not to worry, assuring me that it would come back in after the treatments. He even said it might come back in curlier than before, as if that was going to make me feel better about it.

"Finally, I said to him, 'Don't sweat it, Doc. I hate to lose my hair, but look at it this way. I'm saving a fortune on shampoo!"

At a recent Fun Factor workshop, Harold laughed as he recalled what he said to his doctor who diagnosed his Alzheimer's Disease.

"I told him that at least I'd never again get tired of hearing his old jokes."

9. Use role-reversal techniques in difficult situations

One of the best assets of your humor nature is that it allows you to see things from many different perspectives. This is important because, often, the way to discover the humor in a situation is to turn it up side down or backwards. Anytime you're willing to play with perspective, you're humor nature will meet you more than halfway. It will happily present you with a nearly endless supply of ridiculous alternatives.

The handiest way to practice this mental magic is to get into the habit of playing with time and/or status. For example, imagine what it would be like if there were no time at all. For starters, you would never be late. You wouldn't be too slow or too fast. On the other hand, everything would be happening simultaneously, and that might take some getting used to.

Or, what if time ran backwards? Typical activities might become more humorous. Answers would come before questions (Johnny Carson made a fortune off this premise with Karnack the Magnificent). There would be no mystery in a detective novel. You would start with the results and work back to the problem (Don't we do that sometimes, anyway?). You could jump out of a swimming pool and be dry when you landed on the diving board.

The author of the following joke was simply playing with time:

Question: What happens if you play a country music record

backwards?

Answer: You get your car back, your house back, your dog back …

Another way to play with time is to ask yourself, "What is this situation going to look like 100 years from now?" It takes the pressure off the moment, helps you catch your breath and, of course, gives you some perspective.

The other alternative is to play in your mind with the status or structure of things as you observe them. Everything has a certain hierarchy or order, according to power, value, or preference. If you shift things around, you're likely to discover some fun. For example, the next time you find yourself in a tense confrontation with an authority figure, such as your boss, reverse the roles in your mind. What if she was your employee, but kept acting like she is? Or, if someone is very angrily giving you a piece of his mind, imagine him dressed like a baby, with bonnet and diapers. Mentally playing with status in this way will quite often "even the playing field," when you feel at a disadvantage.

I was on my doctor's examining table waiting for my annual physical examination. Bursting into the room, as if shot from a cannon, came the EKG technician. Obviously she was under some time pressure. Without making eye contact, she muttered a quick, "Good morning," and went immediately to the cardiogram machine.

With her back to me, she started asking for information to write on the EKG tracing.

"Name?"

I told her.

"Age?"

Again, I answered.

"Sex?" she inquired, in a voice that told me she knew that was a silly question.

I paused, and then responded. "Well, OK. But could you lower the lights?"

As we both laughed, there was eye contact for the first time, and the "playing field" became even.

Chapter Nine

THE MORAL AND SPIRITUAL GUIDANCE
OF THE FUN FACTOR

So, here we are. We've learned a lot about the Fun Factor. We've seen how it can produce a fearless family agenda that results in greater self-esteem and self-discipline for all. We've also observed how the basic values of fun-filled family life can play out in the world at large, fueling success and self-fulfillment in the workplace. Then, we have looked at the many ways we can personally maintain the Fun Factor, by developing playful mental habits that keep our humor natures strong and vital.

Shouldn't that be it? Shouldn't we be done? Isn't it time just to put all this into practice, then sit back and enjoy our success and happiness? Thank you very much, Laugh Doctor. It was a great little self-help book.

But it's not that easy.

If by choosing the Fun Factor, we gain more success and satisfaction, what are we to do with what we've gained? Regardless of what measures we choose to gauge our success, even the most global terms, such as "complete and utter satisfaction", or "total happiness" cry out for a context and purpose. Are there goals higher than feeling good and achieving fulfillment?

Suppose you succeed beyond your wildest dreams, which will happen, if you employ the strategies you've learned here. And suppose you are at the pinnacle of happiness and satisfaction, which is also likely to occur. Unless you were to die at that very instant, you would have to make a decision. You would have to decide what to do with your success. You would have to decide how to sustain your satisfaction.

It would be understandable if you decided to preserve that moment. After all, you worked hard to get there. Since you can't imagine a happier moment, what's wrong with trying to make it last as long as possible? Why shouldn't you try to enjoy it for the rest of your life? As reasonable as it sounds, this plan would be a mistake. Life goes on. The moment passes. It is impossible to freeze it and preserve it forever. If you don't let the moment go, life moves on without you, and with it, the joy of living. You would soon find yourself desperately trying to hold onto something you had already lost. You would become filled with fear. You'd begin playing not to lose, when, in reality, the game would already be over. I'll leave it at that, because you already know the limitations of the fear-based strategy, "playing not to lose." This plan would be no fun at all.

But, what is the alternative to this defensive, turf-guarding posture? If we can't bottle up our happiness and preserve it, what hope have we of savoring our successes? This question challenges us to consider what significance there might be in life beyond success and happiness. Perhaps there is something higher and more fulfilling, toward which being successful is just another step. Even though good feeling got us this far, something more seems required to lead us from here. Put another way, if you think you feel good now, you're gonna just love the next step, if you can find it.

Whatever that next step is, we seem to need more than the fleeting satisfaction of success. Success is just not enough. It is not a sufficient end to our efforts. It must lead to something beyond.

What's next after success? This question challenges us to explore the dimensions of life's meaning, significance and ultimate purpose. It puts us into the realm of spirituality. Perhaps to fully enjoy our lives, it is necessary to go beyond knowing what we are, to grapple with the question, "What are we here for?"

From What to Why

We have examined what we are and discovered we are humor beings, possessing a strong humor nature. Now we turn to questions of why. Why do you have a humor nature? Why are you here and who let you in? What can we understand about the overall game plan and our part in it? What does it all mean?

When we start asking those questions, we are entering deep waters. I understand that in these waters, there may be more questions than answers. Still, I encourage you to join me in this exploration, because I don't want to go by myself. If you hold my hand, I'll hold yours, and as long as we're holding hands at least we can't hit each other. While we're at it, we might shed some light on these weighty questions, and, as a result, maybe we could learn to have more fun with our successes. I guess you could say I am inviting you to shift your focus from self-fulfillment to self-enlightenment.

First, let's tackle the question of our humor nature. Why do we have it? The quickest answer is that we have a humor nature because it reflects our humor spirit, but that just leads us around in circles. Another way to get at this might be to look at what our humor nature does for us when it's working well. Much like a high wire walker's pole, its major function seems to be in helping us keep our balance. When we suffer a loss or setback, humor helps us accept it. When we encounter contradictions and incongruities, humor helps us get over them. If we become too caught up in our own sense of self-importance, humor punctures our pomposity. Whenever we're too far down or up, humor gives us perspective. Just as with the ropewalker's pole, humor nature provides everything from a slight shift of perspective to a dramatic counterbalance.

Stay with me here. I think we're on to something. If we have this marvelously effective resource "hardwired" into our nature, and its main function is to keep us in proper perspective, might this not be a clue to our purpose for being here? It leads me to think that our main purpose in life just might be to help each other keep everything in perspective.

I know that doesn't sound like much, but when you stop to think about it, it's a full-time, never-ending job. I don't know about you, but it only takes me a heartbeat to lose my perspective. I need constant counterbalancing or I'll fall off the high wire. If it is my purpose to keep balanced and to help others to do the same, I have no more effective tool than the Fun Factor.

The late Og Mandino, in his best-selling book, *The Greatest Salesman in the World,* agrees. He devotes an entire chapter to humor's power to keep us in balance:

"I will laugh at the world. And with my laughter all things will be reduced to their proper size. I will laugh at my failures and they will vanish in clouds of new dreams; I will laugh at my successes and they will shrink to their true value. I will laugh at evil and it will die untasted; I will laugh at goodness and it will thrive and abound. Each day will be triumphant only when my smiles bring forth smiles from others … To enjoy success I must have happiness, and laughter will be the handmaiden who serves me."

A Spiritual Program

Now we've begun to shed some light on our original question. How do we enjoy a life of success and happiness? We enjoy success by keeping it in perspective and with our humor nature we've got the equipment to do the job. But, even though we understand what it means, keeping perspective is a rather sweeping generalization. How does that actually get done?

One key factor is the element of detachment. This involves a maneuver for which our humor nature is well suited—letting go promptly. It requires discipline, and a constant willingness to loosen our grasp. Like a juggler, if we try to hold onto one ball too long, we will lose the others. By letting go of the one in our grasp, we can catch the next one as it arrives. What we're describing here is a state of ready detachment.

Another key factor is staying in the current moment. This requires focus. We must put on emotional blinders, so that the lingering regrets from the last moment or the anticipation of the next do not distract us. In addition to sharp focus, this takes faith in what is beyond our control.

This introduces surrender, the next component that seems to be necessary for keeping perspective. In order to promptly surrender whatever we have in our grasp, we must acknowledge that we are not in charge, accept that we can't keep control of anything and be continuously willing to release those things we think we are controlling. This is devastating to our egos, but plays to the strength of our humor nature.

The final key to keeping perspective is the capacity to forgive our mistakes by refusing to take ourselves too seriously. If we are not able to allow our humor nature to deal with our self-centeredness, we will quickly lose whatever perspective we have gained.

So now we have defined a spiritual program. We can fulfill our purpose of keeping our perspective and help others keep theirs by: 1) Letting go of our attachments; 2) Staying in the present moment; 3) Giving up control; and 4) Taking ourselves less seriously. Lets take each of these challenges separately and see if we can discover more about the spiritual and moral elements of living a life based on the Fun Factor.

1. Letting go of attachments (Detachment)

The prolific Chinese mystic Tao Te Ching once wrote, "If you realize that all things change, there is nothing you will try to hold on to." Life would be easier for us if we never made any attachments to begin with. Having nothing to lose is the ultimate freedom. Yet, we find it impossible to resist being possessive of the things we value. And whatever we choose to possess, possesses us.

Since we cannot prevent attachments, prompt detachment is our best recourse. Prompt is the operative word here. Whatever time it takes to let go of anything is time spent imprisoned by it. Letting go as quickly as possible is the key to maximum freedom.

When I arrived at the gate for my flight, I encountered a friend whom I had not seen in quite a while. It turned out that she was taking the same flight to attend the same meeting as I. As we sat catching up on old times, it was announced that our departure would be delayed for two hours due to mechanical difficulties.

"Come on," said my friend, charging immediately up to the ticket counter.

I followed her dutifully. We were the first to arrive.

"My friend and I have to be in Orlando tonight. What other arrangements can you make for us?" she inquired.

The agent was reassuring. "This flight will get you there tonight. It will just be two hours later than scheduled."

"Not good enough," quipped my friend. "We need another flight now."

As the agent scrutinized his computer, she whispered to me. "Trust me. I've been through this many times."

Truthfully, I had been reassured by the agent and would have been content to wait out the two-hour delay. But since my friend was indeed a more experienced traveler, I decided to throw in with her.

"The best I can do would be to reroute you through Dallas," the agent offered reluctantly. "You can make a connection there that will get you into Orlando by midnight, but that's an hour and a half later than you'll get there on this flight, even with the delay."

"If there are two seats, we'll take the Dallas option," my friend replied emphatically. "How much time have we got?"

As he printed out our new tickets, the agent warned, "The Dallas flight leaves in 20 minutes. You'll just make it, if you run."

He said nothing more, but his eyes clearly communicated that he thought we were making too much of this minor crisis.

"Make sure our luggage is transferred to the Dallas flight," my friend urged the agent, as we both started running to get to the other gate.

I must admit I was still inclined to think that we were going to a lot of trouble for nothing. It was true that both of us had to be in Orlando by first thing the next morning, but I could see no reason to take a more inconvenient route that would get us there later than the delayed flight. However, it was too late to back out now.

Winded, we settled into our seats on the Dallas flight. Realizing I was a somewhat reluctant participant in her whirlwind reaction, my friend reassured me a second time.

"I've seen this too many times. There's only a fifty-fifty chance that the mechanical problems will get fixed in time. If not, they'll cancel the flight and by that time, there will be no way to get there tonight. We're better off taking the higher odds, even though it's going to take longer."

Of course, I couldn't resist calling the airline the next day to find out what happened to our original flight. It had been cancelled after a second two-hour delay, because the crew was unavailable once the plane was fixed. Without my friend's quick footwork, I might still have been sitting in the airport waiting.

I'm glad I went along with my friend's aggressive plan, but I admit I would never have done it without her. As I think back to my reluctance at the time, part of it had to do with my relative inexperience as an airline traveler. But that wasn't all of it. I remember not wanting to give up the convenience of the original, more familiar, flight. Not only was it to have been a direct flight to Orlando but, even with the proposed delay, it would have gotten me there sooner than the alternative.

In short, I had become "attached" to my original plan. Had it not been for my friend's ability to promptly "detach" on my behalf, I would have been stranded that night. I wonder how many times we unknowingly strand ourselves by failing to detach promptly enough from our expectations.

On a recent family picnic, my four-year-old grandson, William, demonstrated an interesting gesture of prompt detachment. We were having strawberry shortcake for dessert, and my daughter-in-law ran out of strawberries before everyone had been served. William's older brother, Jordan, had not yet gotten his portion.

"Does anybody want to share some of their strawberries so Jordan can have some?" asked my son.

"Here, Jordan," said William, offering all of his strawberries.

"Thank you," chirped Jordan, as he took most of them.

Everyone at the table praised William for his willingness to give up his portion for his brother. He looked proud of himself.

Later, when I was alone with William, I commended him again, telling him how impressed I was that he had been so prompt with his generosity.

William smiled and whispered, "I hate strawberries."

This brings up an important spiritual issue. It's not detachment, if you've never been attached. It's easy to let go of something you deem of no value. That's apathy, not detachment. Becoming apathetic is not the same as surrendering your attachments.

Sometimes we're tempted to build a wall around our hearts to keep from caring about the things and people in our lives. We lose a beloved pet, and in our pain we vow never to get attached to another one. "It's easier not to care," we say. "There's less pain that way."

By thus attempting to free ourselves from our "prison" of attachments, we only succeed in placing ourselves in 'solitary," a more isolated form of confinement. Refusing to care will not produce the perspective you seek for yourself and others.

The spiritual challenge is to care deeply and still be willing to detach promptly. This can be very painful at times, requiring a familiarity with grief. Your humor nature is a valuable asset in grief, but we will not elaborate on it now. Instead, we will devote the entire next chapter to that subject.

2. Staying in the present moment (Faith)

Having discussed surrender, we now turn our attention to the spiritual exercise of faith. It might surprise you to see that word crop up in this context, but I think keeping our focus exclusively on the here and now takes a great deal of faith, and no small amount of trust.

Here's what I mean. In order to focus entirely on the events that are directly before me, I must put on emotional and mental blinders, so that I won't be tempted or distracted by what came before or what's coming next. The temptation can be strong to take a peek in either direction.

By looking back, I can replay the important moments of my life and imagine living them differently. I can convince myself that, "if only I'd thought of saying this," or "if only I had done that differently," the outcome would have been better.

This kind of second-guessing only appears to be worthwhile. All right, I'll grant you that maybe one run-through might teach me something about avoiding similar mistakes in the future. But that's if you assume I know what should have happened in the first place, which, frankly, I don't. Plus, I won't just rehash the incident once, and neither will you. We go over it again and again and again.

And, while that's going on, we're missing out on our lives as they continue to unfold right in front of us. We're missing the moment-by-moment chances to have fun.

George, a 62-year-old grandfather, recovering from prostate cancer, announced to his support group one day, "I've retired my video camera!"

When asked to explain, he answered, "For the last eight years, I've taken that contraption all over, to every event. You name it—the Grand Canyon, Disney World, New York City, birthdays, anniversaries, Christmases—I've got them all on tape. And you know what? Most of them I've never looked at, and I probably never will. They're just taking up space on a shelf in the den."

"But here's the worst part," he continued. "It suddenly dawned on me that I haven't really been a full participant in those events, because I'm always so busy videotaping. Furthermore, to look at them now would mean taking time out of what's going on currently. It looks to me like, by taping everything, I'm getting further and further behind without any hope of ever catching up. So, I've decided to put down the camera and participate in these things as they take place."

"We're going back to Grand Canyon without the camera," he added. "I'm going to see it with my own eyes, not through a viewfinder. This time, I'm going to really be there."

Good for George. He's decided to stop postponing his fun.

I can hear his grandchildren now. "Gee, Grandpa, you sure look different without a camera in front of your face. We never realized you had a moustache!"

While looking back can be a powerful temptation, the urge to look ahead is even stronger. After all, it's been drummed into us since our first Boy Scout campout to "be prepared." Why, it would be downright irresponsible not to look into the future. How else can we adequately equip ourselves for what's coming next?

I think looking ahead can be an even bigger waste of time than looking back. Trying to read the future correctly is daunting enough, but the prospect of addressing tomorrow's imagined problems with resources and knowledge that are barely enough for today, can be overwhelming to the point of paralysis. "Give us this day our daily bread," are the words of an oft-repeated prayer, and a daily portion of bread is just the right amount. We don't need a month's or a year's portion all at one time.

I met Bob at a speaking engagement a few years ago. He had been a well-known Olympic athlete, excelling in his event over several Olympiads. I was thrilled to meet him and while we chatted, I couldn't control my curiosity.

"Bob, you were able to perform at such a high level of excellence over all those years. I'm sure it took great focus and discipline to maintain your edge. Yet, at the same time, your fame must have been a distraction. How were you able to keep the focus you needed to compete at that level for so long?"

"I follow my ten foot rule," he answered. "I learned it when I was a youngster, training in my event. My coach was a demanding so-and-so. We assumed he'd learned to coach in a Nazi concentration camp. He was famous for ending his grueling practices by ordering wind sprints up a very steep hill, not once but several times, at full speed and in quick succession."

"That would literally push me to the limit," he continued. "There were days I didn't think I was going to make it. But, every time I thought of stopping, I would tell myself I could go ten feet further. And I always could make ten more feet. Soon I got in the habit of never looking further ahead than ten feet. And by the time

I'd see the finish line, it would be only ten feet away – a piece of cake.

"Over the years, I've found that, no matter how bad I feel, and no matter what I'm up against, I can do it, if I just take it ten feet at a time. I never look up to see how far I've got to go. I know I can do ten more feet and when I finally see the finish line, it has never been more than ten feet away."

This wisdom of "one day at a time" pervades every major religion and spiritual discipline. But, you might ask, just where does faith come in? It takes faith to let the past rest just as it is, even though you are not certain you did it right. It takes faith to believe that you already have in your possession enough of whatever you need to get through the challenges of this present moment. And it takes faith to trust that the next moment will never find you unprepared, if you allow it to come to you on its own terms.

The faith it takes must be in something or someone capable of shaping and moving the circumstances that you have excluded from your focus; something or someone outside your control. You may choose to rely on chance, fate, science, Higher Power, Buddha, God, or the universe at large. Just be sure that whatever or whomever it turns out to be has a humor nature.

3. Giving up control (Surrender)

The third element of our spiritual program is an elaboration on the first two. Once we commit to a faith that enables us to trust the process of life, and we promptly let go of the things that are beyond our control, we face the issue of interacting on a day-to-day basis with the larger entity upon which we have chosen to rely. For the remainder of this discussion, let's call that larger entity your higher power.

How will we endure the loss of control we experience by constantly letting go? How will we live out the terms of our surrender? Like the chronic smoker said, "Quitting cigarettes is easy. I've done it a hundred times. It's staying off them that's hard." How do we surrender control and stay surrendered?

Barbara, a middle-aged woman recovering from breast

cancer, had a reputation for "hiding" behind intellectualizations during support group meetings. She had been called on this many times and encouraged to get out of her head and into her heart. Admitting that this was her way of controlling her emotions, she had asked the group to help her learn to loosen up.

During one session, she seemed to be getting somewhere. Regarding the topic on the table, she was sharing her feelings in lieu of her thoughts. She was admitting her fears, instead of preaching intellectualized platitudes.

Wishing to support Barbara's efforts, another patient offered reinforcement.

"When I hear you share your feelings like that, I feel closer to you than at any other time. I hope in the future you will continue to speak from your heart instead of your head."

Without hesitation, Barbara answered, "Thank you. I'll really think about that."

Everyone, including Barbara, laughed.

It comes right down to the terms of surrender and what we're really giving up. The terms are simple enough to describe. If we are going to surrender control at all it must be nothing less than unconditional. Otherwise, regardless of appearances, we are retaining control. Surrender becomes meaningless if it is just another ploy to gain the outcome we want. We won't get far with that kind of chicanery. Like pregnancy, surrendering control is an all or nothing proposition.

But, what are we really giving up? We are in fact surrendering only our control over the outcomes of our efforts, something we've never really had anyway. That's it. We continue to retain the prerogative to choose our attitude, demeanor and behavior in each moment of our lives. All we're really promising when we surrender is that we will no longer try to manage the outcomes of our efforts. We intend to stop managing our lives and, instead, live them.

The distinction between managing life and living it warrants further elaboration. We've all heard John Lennon's quote, "Life is what happens while you're making plans." When we refuse to let go of the past and continue to tamper with the future, we are attempting to manage the outcome we want in order to meet our expectations. Once we stop doing that, we are free to simply live our lives, as they unfold.

Another helpful distinction here is that of expectation versus hope. Generally speaking, expectation has to do with our wants, while hope addresses our needs. Since our needs are usually a lot simpler than our wants, it follows that the same could be said of our hopes in relation to our expectations.

In Frank Capra's perennially popular film, *It's A Wonderful Life*, there's a scene in which a panicked crowd of customers storms the bank to withdraw all of their money. Jimmy Stewart's character, realizing that there is not enough cash in the till to satisfy all the demands, comes up with a plan to save the financial integrity of the institution.

He explains that most of the money is not on the premises, since it has been invested in various mortgages and loans. He asks each person to modify his cash demands down to only what he will need for the next day or two. He predicts that if every member will be satisfied with only what she needs, instead of what she wants, they will get through the crisis together, and the Savings and Loan will not have to go out of business.

It takes some cajoling and encouragement, but gradually each member accepts only the money he immediately needs and leaves the rest. In case you are one of the few people on earth not to have seen this film, I'll tell you that they make it through the business day with one dollar to spare.

Surrendering control of our lives does not require us to surrender our hope, only our expectations.

Now, let's look at what you might want to know about the characteristics of the higher power you're surrendering to. You may remember I suggested earlier that, whatever it is, you should make certain it has a humor nature. That's because I think, when we get down to actually surrendering, it's either going to be to fear or to fun. Those are the only choices.

If, for any reason, you surrender to a fear-based higher power, your self-protective instincts will ultimately not allow you to enjoy each moment. You will eventually have to take the blinders off and be on guard against fearful and threatening unknown possibilities. You won't be able to trust life to unfold on its own terms. You'll be forced to manipulate and "manage", with no time left to enjoy, no matter how "successful" you become.

In contrast, by surrendering to the Fun Factor, you will relate to the unknown elements of life with the hope that all of creation reflects the spirit of its creator. If fun characterizes your higher power, you will have no need to be wary of the next moment. You will realize with gratitude that everything that comes to pass will ultimately reflect the very same spirit that inspires your humor nature. You will be assured of always having the personal resources to go "ten feet more."

4. Taking ourselves less seriously (Forgiveness)
The fourth element in our spiritual program is necessary to bring balance to the other three. If you are going to live by the spirit of the Fun Factor, you will need its forgiving power to handle the many times you are going to encounter your own imperfections and those of others. We are all going to frequently fall short of our potential. For example, you will find that, no sooner have you surrendered your expectations, than you have taken them back again, or adopted them under a different guise. It all happens in the blink of an eye, before you are even aware of it.

There is nothing we can do to prevent these precipitous reversals. Actually we need do nothing, if we will stick to the program. The danger is that our mistakes and inconsistencies might tempt us to take matters into our own hands. Whenever we do this, of course we are back to managing our lives. Whether it is damage control or serving penance, it distracts our focus, and take us out of the program.

Much of this loss of focus comes from taking ourselves far too seriously. Who do we think we are that we can refuse to be flexible in light of our inconsistencies? What do we feel we are lacking that we must compensate for by becoming perfectionists? Whatever the answer, I say we need to allow our humor nature to help us get over ourselves.

Do you want to know what I think is going on? I hope you do, because I'm going to tell you anyway. I think we all want to be special. We all want to be unique. We all want to stand out in some way. When I hear somebody say, "But we're all special," I want to answer, "Great! But I want to be even more special than you." There's nothing wrong with this unless we start taking it too seriously.

Here's an image for you:

Imagine standing on a beautiful beach, side-by-side with all humanity. Humor beings are lined up as far as you can see in both directions. We are all holding hands while looking out over the lovely surf to witness the most gorgeous sunset ever. We're all rendered breathless by the beauty. Just as the brilliant sun touches the horizon, you notice that a shimmering reflection of orange light is coming across the water and pointing directly toward you. You think to yourself, "How lucky for me, to be the one person in this entire group to be perfectly aligned with this beautiful shaft of light."

You're feeling pretty special. Then your next thought is, "I wonder if any of the others have noticed who the light is pointing to. If they do, they might be jealous of my position."

Finally, you think, " I'd better not say anything about it. It might make everyone else feel worse."

And, while you having that isolating thought, so is every other person on the beach.

We are all unique. Indeed, we are all special. Your uniqueness doesn't take anything away from mine. And, there seems to be plenty enough for everybody. Just as on the beach, we're all "perfectly aligned." Nobody's getting short-changed.

Where uniqueness is concerned no one is left out. So, let's enjoy the abundance. I don't have to begrudge you yours, nor you mine.

By now, you're thinking I've really lost it, but I haven't, at least not in the way you think. I'm leading up to a discussion of forgiveness, in the strictly spiritual sense of the concept.

In my experience, the spiritual sense of forgiveness has nothing to do with quid pro quo, right versus wrong, or settling of a debt. I'd rather leave those power wielding aspects of forgiveness to be sorted out by the more religious amongst us. I believe forgiveness simply means what the printed word says—to for-give.

To me, this means, if I am forgiving, I am both for giving and for giving first. A forgiving person is in favor of giving, as well as eager to be the first one to give. Let's look at those traits one at a time.

What makes a person for giving? Once again we're back to one of two motivations—fear or fun. We give either out of fear/guilt, or out of joy/satisfaction. Altruism notwithstanding, giving is difficult when we have nothing to spare, but fun when we have more than we need. So, our first answer would be that we are more for giving when we sense we have an abundance or even an overabundance.

Something else is likely to stir us to be more in favor of giving. Somewhere along the way, if we have subscribed to the Fun Factor, we may notice that the more we give away, the more we seem to have. This is a phenomenon noted by many to be a universal spiritual truth. You literally accumulate more by giving than by keeping or hoarding. It can reach a point at which you aren't able to give away fast enough to prevent increased accumulation in your own storeroom. This is another reinforcement for giving. Of course it's selfish, but don't forget we have already established that being selfish is a healthy trait, as opposed to being self-centered.

It is no secret that Jerry Lewis gives hundreds of hours of his time each year to the Muscular Dystrophy Association, and has done so for over fifty years. He calls it the most selfish thing he does.

"Nobody gets more out of it than I do," he says unabashedly. "I am the most selfish man in the organization."

The second element in forgiveness is a willingness to give first. This means, by forgiving, we give every person or situation the "benefit of the doubt" beforehand. I give you my trust, without your having to earn it, and I continue to extend it to you until you give me a reason not to. Similarly, I wish you well, unless you give me cause not to.

I make myself "vulnerable" first, because I have surrendered to the Fun Factor and have no reason to believe you will not share that commitment as well. Since whatever I give to you is what I am likely to get back from you, if I initiate our relationship with fear and guardedness, that is how you will treat me. If, however, I assume you are committed to fun, you are more likely to assume the same of me.

Regarding so-called transgressions, I will recognize in myself the propensity to make mistakes and I will render myself accountable to each mistake as a lesson to teach me a better way. Therefore I will not hold myself in contempt for my inconsistencies, nor attempt to punish myself when I am wrong. Instead I will encourage myself to make swift amends, and to integrate my newfound knowledge into positive growth. I will respond to your transgressions in the same manner, as long as you are willing to be similarly accountable.

Inspired by the Fun Factor, we can choose to see only the good in one another. And, by remaining detached, faithful, surrendered and forgiving, we will find an abundance of joy within us that will multiply in the sharing.

That is how we can live with our successes.

Chapter Ten

THE FUN FACTOR AMID GRIEF AND TRAGEDY

It was the most devastating moment of my life.

I was sitting at my desk, writing a letter, when the phone rang. As I answered, I heard a familiar voice on the line, and I could tell something was dreadfully wrong.

"Cliff, this is your sister-in-law, Ruth. I have some bad news. Your brother Doug was killed this morning in an automobile accident."

Her words exploded in my brain with such stunning force that I was immobilized, physically and mentally. NO! NO! NO! NO! NO is all I remember thinking and saying. This couldn't be true. It must be a dream. It had to be a mistake, or a cruel hoax, anything but the truth.

Trying to breathe was the first order of business. I couldn't.

"Head-on collision ... 7 AM ... on his way to school ... no details ... I'm in shock." All I could hear were brief phrases.

Ouch! Ouch! Oh my God! I wanted to scream, but I couldn't —or wouldn't.

Then came the guilt, for me the constant companion of helpless moments. What could I have done? What should I have done? I should have protected him better. It's my fault. I'm the older brother. I should have been there. I'm sorry for everything, anything. Please forgive me, anybody. Help! Help! It hurts too much.

"Oh God, I'm sorry. Ruth, I'm so sorry. What will we do?"

What a call to receive at any time. But two days before Christmas, it was especially difficult. It has been eight years since that moment, and the memory is still so vivid and painful, it is difficult to write about it.

My younger brother's death is, up to this moment, my most traumatic experience with grief. To get through it, I could do nothing except hold onto the living persons near me, cry, pray and, eventually, thank God, laugh again.

I know I'm not unique. We have all felt, directly or indirectly, the sting of grief. We know it can be a shockingly dramatic and painful intrusion into our lives, upsetting our sense of control and balance and confronting us with our frail vulnerability and helplessness. In a recent workshop, one participant stated that an aunt and a best friend were both dying of cancer at the same time. Another had lost three grandparents and a father in one year. A third person described losing both parents and her twin daughters in less than 12 months. And a fourth reported her mother-in-law diagnosed with liver cancer, her uncle diagnosed with cancer of the larynx and her grandmother with cirrhosis, all in the same week.

Dramatic grief demands our full attention and literally has its way with us. Day after interminable day it holds us hostage to wrenching pain and fear. Try as we might, we cannot get around it. We must endure it until it runs its course.

But, that's not the way most of our grief visits us. More frequently, grief comes upon us quietly and without fanfare. This kind of grief is so common that it slips beneath our radar. We hardly notice it or the toll it takes on us. I'm referring to the grief each one of us experiences every day in response to constant change in our lives.

Change is inevitable—except from a vending machine! This familiar bumper sticker reflects the truth. As much as we may hate to acknowledge it, the only thing constant in life is change.

And every change—large or small, dramatic or subtle—

forces us to give up what's familiar for something unknown and less familiar. This takes its mental and physical toll, even if the change is a welcome one. The problem is, when it comes to change, we don't get to choose between welcome and unwelcome.

So, change means only one thing to us— loss. When familiar things are taken from us, the loss has many faces; loss of control, loss of comfort, loss of status, loss of security, loss of freedom, loss of choice, loss of function, loss of acceptance, loss of connection, loss of pleasure and even loss of love.

It is thus natural and understandable that we resist change strenuously. We dig in our heels and refuse to budge an inch. Or we find something or someone to blame and launch an attack on the "cause" of our distress. In the worst cases, we try to ignore the change and go on as if nothing were different.

These tactics never work. Change just keeps on happening, no matter what we think of it. Plus, as we have already seen, when we dig in our heels, we jeopardize our own health and happiness. In other words, we are the ones who suffer the most from our resistance to change.

Finding resistance fruitless, we have no choice but to face the daily losses that are taking place in our lives. When we do, we come immediately and inevitably back to grief. Grieving is the only tool we humor beings have for dealing with our losses. For all its pain and discomfort, grief is a normal and healthy human reaction. Nonetheless, we do not find it appealing.

I have some good news. As I hinted in the last chapter, you and I have an unlikely resource available to help us with our grief, both large and small. But, it is a resource we must remember to use.

What resource am I talking about? Humor. That's right. Even though we don't ordinarily associate grieving with fun, your humor nature offers many benefits to you when you're in grief. We will elaborate shortly, but, first, I would like to tell you how I came to know this. Like most of the truly valuable lessons I've learned about the Fun Factor, this one came from a cancer patient:

Less than a month after she learned the persistent pain in her right leg was a tumor called sarcoma, 15-year-old Darla had sought my help. Her oncologist had told her she had only 18 months to live, but she informed me right off the bat that she was planning to go on much longer than a year and a half.

Darla had heard about some cancer patients who had been successful using relaxation and imagery to reinforce the effect of their chemotherapy treatments. She wanted to learn how to do that and she wanted to start immediately, if not sooner.

Our work together spanned more than five years until her death at age twenty. Those years were filled with many incredible moments for Darla—high school graduation, college, romance, marriage, a honeymoon in Hawaii and lots of laughter. In that time Darla taught me many things.

The most important lesson she taught me was to laugh during serious moments. I had always "approved" of humor, but only in its place and time, which was after all responsibilities had been met. I was a serious doctor of medicine.

Darla maintained that if we waited for my criteria to be met, we might never laugh. She thought laughter's place was everywhere, and its time, any time.

Her sense of humor took no prisoners. It was audacious and spontaneous.

For example, once, after she had lost her hair from chemotherapy, she had the following interaction with her brother Craig, who was two years younger than she.

Both were helping their mother hang some curtains. Craig took a valance from Darla and chauvinistically climbed the ladder, saying, "You better let somebody strong do this."

"Oh Yeah?" Darla retorted. "Well, I can do something you can't!"

"What's that?" Craig asked.

"This!" was her reply.

With that, Darla hooked her forefinger under her wig and lifted it off her head, twirling it in the air.

At the time she recounted this to me in my office, she demonstrated the wig twirling. It was one of the funniest things I have ever seen. Her hairless scalp was shining, her eyes were sparkling and a triumphant grin beamed from her face.

We laughed together breathlessly for more than a minute. It is an image I'll never forget.

This is not a case of laughing away unwanted fears and burdens, making light of a painful experience or avoiding serious issues. Darla's cancer was very real and very serious. It took her life at age 20.

Instead, it is an account of a remarkable young lady choosing to live the years she was given by transcending her fears and pain. Even after reading the chapter on spirituality, you may think that transcendence is too mystical a concept to be used in describing the day-to-day struggles of living. But it is the right word for what we're talking about. Darla literally rose above her fear and pain.

Don't confuse what she did with avoidance. Transcendence is very different from avoidance. In avoidance, we ignore, deny or otherwise skirt an unwanted experience. In transcending it, we acknowledge fear and pain, but maintain a perspective that prevents those elements from disabling us.

Also, if you are tempted to surmise that Darla got cheated out of life, that's because you did not know her. She packed more living into her twenty years than most of us will manage in four times that long.

What was her secret? She understood her humor nature — what it was and what it was for.

In a term paper written for her English Composition course, during freshman year in college, Darla wrote: "... a sense of humor goes beyond the ability to tell an amusing anecdote and includes a capacity to see the positive aspects of otherwise adverse situations. I use my own sense of humor to help me remain sane through the difficult times in my battle with cancer."

Nobody checked with Darla to see if she was agreeable to a cancer diagnosis. No one sat down with her to work out a negotiated settlement or a transition plan. Her losses could not be resolved or compensated. She had to transcend them or become mired in resentment, self-pity and despair.

Come to think of it, most of life's important transitions are like that. There is little that can be negotiated. Even when conflict resolution or other forms of assistance provide some quid pro quo, it is impossible to resolve everything. We walk away with less than we hoped for, and our going forward is usually constrained by certain conditions. If we're to get past our lingering resentments and disappointments, we must learn to rise above them.

How Darla figured this out at such a tender age, I do not know. All I can tell you is that she was a brilliant example of the Fun Factor as it applies to grief. For all of us involved in her care, she became a "walking textbook" of humor nature. For me, she was, and still remains, an inspiration for the research I have pursued to gain the information I'm going to share with you about humor's role in grief.

What worked for Darla will work for any of us. We, too, can transcend loss and sustain a quality of life never deemed possible under the circumstances of change in our lives. We can facilitate our own grief and move beyond it. It only requires learning to appreciate, respect and trust the Fun Factor as Darla did.

Fun and Grief

First, let me reiterate that grief, despite its discomfort, is a thoroughly normal and healthy response to any frustrated expectation, a response that is necessary for health and success. Our goal should not be to avoid it, because that can never be accomplished. Rather, we should strive to expedite our grieving, so that we are held back as little as possible by it. This ties in with our earlier discussion of the wisdom of letting go promptly. To understand how the Fun Factor can help us in this effort, we must first be reminded of how grief works under normal conditions.

The purpose of grief is quite simply to help us accept, and thus adapt to, any loss. It accomplishes this by virtue of three mechanisms:

1. Releasing what is gone.
2. Expressing emotion about the loss
3. Accepting new circumstances

Let's elaborate upon the three actions involved—releasing, expressing and accepting. They will take on added importance later, as we consider the Fun Factor's role in grief.

Releasing or letting go
When we suffer a loss, the first order of business is to release our grip on the things we've lost. There is no way to move beyond the pain until we do.

Expressing emotion or ventilation
If we try to bottle up pain and fear, it will drain any energy we might have available for adapting to our loss. We must rid ourselves of the burden of strong, pent-up emotions before we can move forward.

Accepting or facing facts
We cannot go on beyond our loss until we can accept the altered options left to us in its wake. Acceptance is the first step in any healing process.

The process by which these actions of grief are carried out is fairly uniform in each of us. By now everyone is familiar with the Stages of Grief as delineated by Kubler-Ross and her colleagues. Stereotypically, grief moves through five phases—Denial, Anger, Bargaining, Depression and Acceptance:

Denial
When change/loss occurs, our first reaction is to deny it. We will close our eyes, question the reliability of the facts, and sometimes even run away. It appears we would rather do almost anything but acknowledge a loss. When denial fails to change the reality, we move to our second line of defense.

Anger
Unable to deny the facts, we next resort to intimidation. Like the mythical rulers of old, we threaten to kill the messenger

because we don't like the message. We rail at the universe in the vain attempt to reverse our misfortune. When this doesn't get us anywhere, we move to a third strategy.

Bargaining

Noting that reality is not influenced by our rage, we attempt a more conciliatory posture. Perhaps if we are willing to give up part of what we have lost, the balance will be restored to us. After all, half a loaf is better than none. Of course, since we've already lost, we have no leverage. When bargaining doesn't work either, it is as though the last barrier falls and we are left with no choice but to feel the full brunt of the loss.

Depression/Sadness

Depression is the term Kubler-Ross designated for this stage. As a psychiatrist, I would not use it here, because I consider depression a pathological event, requiring medical treatment. Since I do not believe grief is a pathologic process, I would prefer the term sadness. Regardless of what you may call it, this is the most painful stage of grief, and the one most commonly identified with it. We cry, we lose our appetites, we withdraw socially, and we may even develop health problems.

Acceptance

After spending sufficient time in the sadness phase (which always lasts longer than we would like), we emerge into a state of acceptance of our loss. This term may be the most misunderstood in common parlance. Acceptance does not mean endorsement or approval. It does not require that we are happy with, or even like, the situation. Acceptance simply means the acknowledgement of things as they are, like them or not. It is when we reach this state of acceptance that we are ready to *begin* rebuilding our lives after a loss. The entire grief process amounts to only the first step in healing, not its culmination.

In this brief overview of grief we have described a personal ritual, common to all of us, by which we find it possible to let go, express ourselves, and ultimately come to acceptance of something we started off trying to avoid. What has humor got to do with this? None of it sounds like fun.

But, wait. Isn't humor a personal ritual? Isn't it common to us all, in that we all possess humor nature? Doesn't humor encourage us to let go and express ourselves? And haven't we seen the Fun Factor help make unpleasant situations more acceptable? Why, if I didn't know we were talking about humor, I might think we were referring back to grief. There are many parallels here. It's surprising how much common ground grief and humor appear to share.

If we look more closely, we will see that the Fun Factor not only shares the same mechanisms as grief, but also fits into the same process. First, let's look at the three mechanisms we discussed – releasing, expressing and accepting—but, this time from the point of view of humor.

Releasing/Letting Go

Robert Fulghum, in his book, *It Was on Fire When I Laid Down on It*, wrote, "Tears bring relief, but laughter brings release." Having fun is the ultimate in letting go. Our humor nature is always ready to come forward and energize the situation, just as soon as we get out of the way. It is impossible to laugh without letting go. Believe me. I tried and it gave me a hernia.

Expressing/Ventilating

We've identified fun as pure energy. It doesn't require extended rationalization. As a free and spontaneous expression of emotion, it's as simple as it gets. That is why we often regard laughter as a good "icebreaker." When we are guarded, humor gets emotion flowing and reassures us that, despite perceived differences, we have much in common.

Because it's so beneficial to the free expression of emotion, we find humor prevalent in such grief rituals as Irish wakes and the assignment of "joke partners" for the bereaved in the African Tiwi culture.

Accepting

Resistance to the unfamiliar makes acceptance difficult. Therefore, it follows that anything that makes the unfamiliar more appealing will help. All humor is based to some extent on the unexpected—a surprise. When asked why people laughed at their shows, 65 percent of professional comedians responded, "They laugh because I surprise them."

A surprise is a form of frustrated expectation. We enjoy surprises. Hence fun makes us more accepting of the unexpected and unfamiliar.

Well, so far our humor nature meets every qualification to assist in grief's mechanisms. Let's see how fun might be a welcomed adjunct to the various stages of the process.

Actually, even before the identifiable grief process begins, the Fun Factor can help us. We never know when unwanted news is going to arrive. If we have cultivated a strong and reliable humor attitude, it will serve as a residual "shock absorber", which can soften the blow, obviating the need for a stronger denial to start with. Remember, our goal should always be to shorten the time necessary to get through grief.

Denial

There is much material for humor in denial. Think of the fable, "The Emperor's New Clothes." Can you imagine how ridiculous he looked, walking around in his altogether, thinking he had clothes on? We can create the same impression, when we're in denial. We aren't really fooling anyone but ourselves.

For many years I was a regular guest on a radio call-in show, appearing once or twice a month to discuss various topics related to mental health. It was the custom each summer for the radio station to hire a group of interns, usually students from local colleges who were interested in getting a "taste" of working on the radio.

One summer, one of the interns was a charming young lady named Heather. Heather was beautiful, vivacious, friendly, and—well, I'll just cut to the bottom line. I thought Heather was great, because she thought I was terrific.

"Oh, Dr. Kuhn, I just love the way you handle those calls on the air with sensitivity and compassion, and you always say something positive to give the person hope," Heather would gush on. "Whenever you're on the air, I want to be in the studio to observe your technique."

I had a tough time resisting that kind of attention from a gorgeous young lady.

"Of course, Heather," I would reply, "I'm happy to have you join us when I'm on the air. Come in anytime."

You see, I'm not a dirty old man. But, I'm not dead yet, either. Let's just say I was always happy to see Heather, and leave it at that.

One evening during that summer, we had completed the first hour of our three-hour show, and had broken for the news. I said to my host," I'm going to the men's room. I'll be right back." "Better hurry," he replied. "This is a short break."

So, I rushed out of the studio and was running down the hall, when I spotted Heather coming in the opposite direction. I immediately slowed down to a more nonchalant pace.

Upon seeing me, she exclaimed, "Oh, I forgot you were on tonight, Dr. Kuhn. As soon as I finish this work, I want to come in and observe the second hour."

"You come right ahead, as soon as you can," I told her, as we came nearly face-to-face, and she gave me that smile of hers that always quickened my step. "I'll be looking for you."

As we passed in the hall, I reached for the men's room door and opened it. But, when I turned to go in, I realized that I hadn't opened the men's room door. I had mistakenly opened the door of the broom closet next to the men's room.

Well, I didn't want Heather to notice my little mistake, so, guess what I did. I walked on into the broom closet and let the door close behind me. I figured, Heather would walk on down the hall and, once she was out of sight, I could correct my error privately and without embarrassment.

I stood silently in the dark broom closet for a few seconds. When I decided the coast was clear, I tried to let myself out and that's when the trouble started. The door would not open from the inside. I was trapped in the broom closet!

To my credit, I didn't panic. I figured that the hall was traveled frequently enough that someone passing by would hear me if I simply kept knocking softly on the door. So I began knocking. After what seemed like hours, but was in reality only a couple of minutes, the door burst open. It was the host of the call-in show.

"Cliff," he exclaimed, "what are you doing in the broom closet?"

"It's a long story," I mumbled. "How did you know I was here?"

"Heather told me," was his reply.

Now, I ask you, who was I fooling with my cover-up? Certainly not Heather.

One of my favorite cartoons is of two prisoners, chained helplessly side by side, high on the prison wall. One is whispering to the other, "OK. Now here's the plan." Denial is funny.

Not to mention the proverbial posture associated with denial —"burying our heads in the sand." Do you realize that when your head is buried in the sand a certain part of your anatomy remains most exposed? Picture that the next time you think about denial, and you might smile.

Anger

Don't tell me there's nothing humorous about anger. Next time you're enraged, take a look in the mirror. Your face is red, your eyes are bulging, the veins on your forehead are puffed up and you're salivating like a rabid chipmunk. If you ever want to stop an argument in mid-sentence, hold up a mirror.

Another place for humor in anger is the amusement that generates from missing the mark. Anger will often propel us past the desired "target," into saying and doing things that we never intended. This is the exaggerated stuff of slapstick humor.

During one of our "Laughter and Healing" seminars, Jerry Lewis was illustrating the subtle humor of missing the mark, by pouring a glass of water from a pitcher on the table, while continuing to talk. He kept talking, and pouring, even after the glass was full, so that the audience could see it overflowing onto the table, "unbeknownst" to Jerry, who just kept pouring. Everyone found it very funny.

Moments later, Jerry was standing in front of the table, engaged in dialogue with a member of the audience. As he listened intently to her comment, he leaned back and sat on the table, apparently forgetting the spilled water, which had not been wiped up. It took just a second or two for the puddle to seep through the seat of his pants. As soon as he felt it, he jumped up in surprise, evoking an even stronger laugh from the audience than before.

He swore the second "missed mark" (sitting in the puddle) was unintentional. Knowing Jerry Lewis, we all had our doubts.

If you ever doubt that humor belongs with anger, think of Jackie Gleason's character, Ralph Cramden, in *The Honeymooners*. "To the moon, Alice. To the moon!"

Bargaining

Jerry Lewis defines comedy simply as "a man in trouble." There is indeed something amusing about the irrepressible optimism of someone who, on the brink of inevitable defeat, attempts to leverage some advantage. We've heard the saying, "beggars can't be choosers," nearly all our lives, yet we can't resist a smile. Picture the three-year-old child at bedtime, boldly offering to go obediently, if he is allowed to stay up another fifteen minutes.

Or there is the desperate bargaining portrayed in this joke:

A mother called her daughter on the phone, and surmised by her tone of voice that the day was not going well.

"I can tell by your voice something's wrong," she said. "Tell mama what's going on. Maybe I can help."

"You won't believe it, Ma," replied the daughter. "Both the kids are running fevers, the house is a mess and, just before you called the oven stopped working, so our dinner is ruined."

"I'll come right over," offered the mother. "Don't worry. I'll get the kids settled and we can figure out what to do about dinner."

"You mean it?" asked the daughter. "That would save the day, because Harry is bringing his boss home for dinner tonight.

"Harry?" asked the mother. "Who's Harry?"

"Harry's my husband, Ma. What a silly question," replied the voice on the phone.

"Who is this?" the mother demanded.

"Ma, it's your daughter Sylvia," was the response.

"My daughter's name is Susan," declared the mother. "I'm sorry. I must have dialed a wrong number."

"Does that mean you won't be coming over to help?"

Last-ditch bargaining has much potential for humor. Add to that the observation that things are often more negotiable when we are having fun, and you have built a strong role for the Fun Factor in this stage of grief.

Depression/Sadness

You would think there is not much room for humor in this stage of grief, but here are a few testimonials that might make you think again:

"I have seen what laughter can do. It can transform almost unbearable tears into something bearable, even hopeful."

−Bob Hope

"It is incredible how much happiness, even how much gaiety, we sometimes had together after all hope was gone."

− C. S. Lewis: A Grief Observed

"I am always aware that Charlie is playing with death. He plays with it, mocks it, thumbs his nose at it, but it is always there. He is aware of death at every moment of his existence."

− Charles Chaplin

"Funny had better be sad somewhere."

− Jerry Lewis

Since fun is not of our making, it already exists in every circumstance, whether or not we choose to acknowledge it. Therefore it can emerge at the most unlikely moments, offering dramatic and inexplicable comfort and assurance.

A young graduate student at the seminary agreed to fill in as pastor at a small rural church, while the regular pastor took an eight-week leave. Although the student had previously done some preaching, this was to be his first experience at actually serving as the "shepherd of the flock."

Within days of his arrival, a tragedy struck the congregation. The teenage daughter of a prominent church family was killed instantly in an automobile accident.

On the morning of the mishap, the student went with fear and trepidation to the home of the stricken family, feeling helpless to offer much, but knowing he should be there. He was admitted to the home and immediately saw the father and siblings in the living room, being comforted by friends and neighbors.

The father looked up, recognized the young pastor, and said, "We're OK. Go to her." And he pointed upstairs.

At that moment, the pastor became aware of the most heart-wrenching wailing he had ever heard, coming from the second floor. He followed the pitiful sound up the stairs, uncertain as to what he would find. It led him to a bedroom where the mother was lying supine on her bed with eyes closed, wailing out the pain of her broken heart.

Her incessant wailing precluded him from announcing his arrival. So, he simply walked quietly to her bedside, reached down, and gently took her hand. The mother seized his hand and held it tightly. But she did not open her eyes, nor did she interrupt her wailing.

The pastor thought to himself, "At least I've made some contact. She will know someone is with her." He decided to simply wait, squatting down beside the bed, maintaining the contact.

The woman went on sobbing and her eyes remained closed. After several minutes in his squatting position, the pastor's legs began to ache. Not wanting to break the hand-to-hand contact, he glanced quickly behind him and saw what he thought was a closed closet door. He thought if he could just lean back against the door, it would get the weight off his aching legs.

As he leaned back, he realized, too late, it was not a closet door. It was a bathroom door and it opened inward, giving way behind him. He lost his balance and fell over backwards into the bathroom, breaking the physical contact he had been so carefully preserving.

The wailing stopped. As the pastor looked up from the floor, he saw the woman sitting upright on the bed looking down at him. She burst into laughter, which lasted perhaps ten or fifteen seconds, then stopped abruptly. She immediately lay back down, closed her eyes and resumed her sobbing as before.

The pastor got up, brushed himself off and went downstairs, convinced he had failed mightily in his attempt to be comforting. Thereafter, he carried through with all his pastoral responsibilities, leading the appropriate ceremonies and rituals, and everything went well, considering the circumstances. But he continued to feel awful about his clumsy faux pas.

Weeks later he was attending a farewell party given at the church on the eve of his departure, when the grieving mother approached him haltingly.

"I'm sorry I haven't spoken to you before this," she said tearfully, "but I just couldn't let you leave without thanking you for everything, especially what you did for me on the morning my daughter was killed."

"What was it that I did?" he asked cautiously.

She answered, "When you fell into our bathroom, you made me laugh. And the laughter gave me hope that I would get through the pain."

Acceptance

I truly believe humor is a form of acceptance and, conversely, acceptance is an expression of humor or joy. When we are having fun, we find it easier to accept things as they are, and our acceptance then adds to our fun.

A funeral can play a major role in our grief process over the death of a friend or loved one. By formally laying the deceased person "to rest," we seek some acceptance of the finality of our loss. However, even this solemn event can harbor life-affirming humor.

A minister friend tells this story. An elder of his church had died and on the eve of his funeral, the congregation had gathered for a vigil at the widow's home. It being a small dwelling, the crowd filled the house almost beyond capacity.

During the evening, my friend mentioned to the widow that he would like a quiet moment with her to review his plans for the next day's funeral. She appreciated his offer, but the only quiet place to be found was a small bathroom adjacent to the living room. They went in and closed the door.

The widow sat on the edge of the bathtub and the pastor sat on the commode, seat down, of course. They went over the proposed ceremony. The widow was pleased and grateful, approving everything.

Before ending their brief meeting, the pastor suggested a word of prayer. They held hands while he prayed.

As he said, "Amen," they both arose from their makeshift seats. That was when the pastor's right hand, with a mind all its own, reached back and flushed the commode. It was done before he could stop it.

There they stood facing each other, embarrassed by the flushing sound enveloping them. Certainly it was loud enough to be heard by those in the adjacent room.

Recognizing they couldn't spend the rest of the evening "hiding" in the bathroom, and thinking it would be somewhat undignified for them to crawl out the window, my friend took the initiative and opened the door. They both walked boldly out into the curious stares of the congregation.

~

We were returning from the cemetery, following the graveside service of my father's funeral. Riding in the limousine were my mother, my brother, my sister-in-law, my wife and me. We were silent for a few minutes, then my brother spoke up.

"Cliff, did you notice how the casket hit the side of the grave as it was being lowered into the ground?" he asked.

"Yes," I answered, "I heard it hit before I saw it."

"Isn't that just like Dad?" he continued. "Slapstick to the end."

That comment got us all thinking about the way Dad had always lightened the most serious moments with a bit of spontaneous silliness.

"He never left a room without 'accidentally' walking into the wall," my brother reminisced.

"And how about his entrances?" I countered. "He would always 'trip' over the edge of a rug and break into an exaggerated jog to cover his miscue."

Soon everyone was contributing similar memories, about the way he used to hum to cover accidental body noises, or how, if you caught him picking at his nose, he would pretend to be looking closely at his watch, or his silly way of dancing. Before we knew it, we were all laughing uncontrollably, grateful heirs to Dad's legacy of fun.

When we got out of the limo, our tear-stained faces were smiling. We were a fun-filled fearless family.

Dad wouldn't have wanted it any other way.

My friend Steven was near death. As a gynecologic surgeon, he had spent his entire professional life heroically "saving" women from the clutches of cancer. By some cruel irony of fate, he was succumbing, after a valiant personal struggle, to his own cancer.

I sat at his bedside in the hospital room, aware that this was likely to be the last time I saw him alive. Wracked with pain and nearly comatose from medication, he was awaiting his discharge from the hospital, in honor of his wish to die at home.

As I watched him sleep I was thinking, if they didn't discharge him quickly, he wouldn't make it home to die.

He opened his eyes and looked at me. There were no words. I could tell he was glad to see me. He could tell I was grateful for a few quiet moments with him. No words were needed.

I broke the silence first.

"Well, Steven, I've got to be going."

"Can't take it, eh?" he challenged me gently.

"Well, this is difficult, but that's not it," I explained. "I have to give a lecture to the second year students."

"Oh yeah? What are you going to lecture about?" He was keeping me honest.

"I'm lecturing on the doctor-patient relationship," I answered. "If there's anything you would like me to say to them, I'd be happy to quote you."

His eyes lit up. For as long as I had known Steven, teaching had been his greatest passion.

He thought for a few seconds, and then said, "Yeah. Tell them two things for me. First, always tell your patient the truth. And, second – never ask a patient to do something you're not willing to do yourself."

I broke out laughing.

"What are you laughing at?" he asked.

"That last one is funny," I answered, thinking of how women had to put their feet in stirrups for a gynecologic examination. "Those are strange words coming from a male gynecologist, who has never had his feet in the stirrups."

He got the picture and we laughed together.

That was our good-bye. Steven died at home the next day. I will always be comforted by the memory of his laughter.

Loss is tough. The world plays for keeps and we are not in charge. Usually we're not even consulted.

Change crashes our party like a rude uninvited guest and we must put up with it. If it's not one thing, it will be something else. As Roseanne Roseanna-danna used to say, "It's always something." These realities are painful, frightening and infuriating.

But we now know that's not the whole story. Even though we can't control the circumstances or avoid the pain, we can do more than merely tolerate the changes in our lives.

We have identified a reliable personal resource for more than mere surviving. And we see how that resource doesn't desert us in our toughest moments. We know we possess the power to rise above our vulnerability and at times actually come out ahead.

That power is the Fun Factor. It is unleashed by our humor nature, when we practice the principles and strategies we've learned in this book. Embracing the Fun Factor, we will realize that, although at times we do not have everything we *want,* we always have everything we *need* to rise above any fear or adversity. Humor nature never fails to respond when we call upon it.

I encourage you to put the fun strategies you have learned into daily practice in your home, at work and in your life. As you do, you will discover the deepest humor truth of all, namely that the essential ingredients for personal success and happiness are contained within yourself, not in the things that are changing all around you. You will realize that, despite the daunting or painful challenges that confront you, nothing can defeat you!

You can live happily over laughter.